Totally God's

Megan Clinton
with her dad, Dr. Tim Clinton

HARVEST HOUSE PUBLISHERS

EUGENE, OREGON

Cover by Koechel Peterson & Associates, Inc., Minneapolis, Minnesota

Cover photo © Izabela Habur / iStockphoto

TOTALLY GOD'S
Copyright © 2008 by Megan Clinton
Published by Harvest House Publishers
Eugene, Oregon 97402
www.harvesthousepublishers.com

Library of Congress Cataloging-in-Publication Data
  Clinton, Megan, 1990-
  Totally God's / Megan Clinton with Tim Clinton.
    p. cm.
  ISBN-13: 978-0-7369-2128-2 (pbk.)
  ISBN-10: 0-7369-2128-1
  1. Teenage girls—Religious life. 2. Teenage girls—Psychology. I. Clinton, Timothy E., 1960- II. Title.
  BV4551.3.C45 2008
  248.8'33—dc22

                                              2008011720

Printed in the United States of America

      08 09 10 11 12 13 14 15 16 / VP-SK / 11 10 9 8 7 6 5 4 3 2 1

This book is dedicated to God's glory,
to Mom and Dad for your love and encouragement
and for challenging me to pursue God's dream for my life,
and to all the young women who want to live freely in Christ
and pursue God's dreams for their lives.

Acknowledgments

Growing up, my Dad taught me that it takes a lot of hard work to succeed and perseverance to finish well. While writing *Totally God's,* I learned my lesson. I had no idea that so much work went into a project like this! There are so many people to thank.

First, I want to thank my heavenly Father for all He has done for me—for giving me such a loving family and this opportunity to share the love and majesty of a God who loves each of us unconditionally with young women everywhere.

A special thank you to Joshua Straub, "my older brother," for the many nights you sat with me to brainstorm and share funny memories. Thank you for helping me with the research, editing, and writing.

Likewise, a special thanks to the Harvest House team—specifically Carolyn McCready and Terry Glaspey for believing in me and giving me this opportunity and Hope Lyda for working hard with me throughout the editing process.

To Tom Winters and his assistant, Debbie Boyd, a huge thanks for introducing me to the publishing world.

I also want to thank my best friend, Jocelyn Bowers, for your support and loyalty through the years. I thank God every day for you. You're the best. And my cousin, Kaelynn Queen, who is basically like my sister, thank you for always being there and sharing your life with me. You are so appreciated.

To all of my friends, thank you for the incredible fun and memories throughout the school years.

A special thanks to my little brother, Zach, for your love, support, and the many, many laughs we share in life together. You are such a joy.

And finally thank you, Mom and Dad, for your love, prayers, and emotional support. I can always count on you to encourage and challenge me to live God's dream for my life. I love you both more than you'll ever know.

Contents

❀

The Journey

God notices things your mother has never even thought about.

–JOHN ORTBERG

I love my mom, but she's about as paranoid as any mother with a teenager ready to get a driver's license. If you're there now or have been through it, you know what I'm talking about. If you're not there yet, just wait! Fun times!

It is so hard to breathe calmly and drive down the road with your mother in the seat next to you. Not because you're afraid of what she'll say, but because she just gasped all of the breathable air out of the car when she thought you had a near miss with a truck that was two lanes away! I don't get it.

Even though it took her a while to allow me to drive back and forth to school by myself, I'm not so sure it was because she didn't trust me. For my mom I know it was more about how hard it was emotionally to watch the little girl she used to braid pigtails for walk out the door every day. That little girl now has her own hairstyle, fashion, makeup, and, heaven forbid, her own car. My mom doesn't want to see her little girl grow up. Just as she had to say goodbye to pigtails and bows, she knows there are parts of her little girl (that would be me) that are changing. But the one thing she doesn't want to change, and neither do I, is our relationship. We both long for that to stay solid.

I think it's this way for God too. He knows us as His kids, His daughters. He knows every single little detail about you—the Bible says He even knows the number of hairs on your head. And because He knows you so well, even better than you know yourself, He, like your mom, wants to protect you. To be there for you. He wants to do all He can to make sure you are His girl and that He never loses one part of you.

What scares me is the number of girls I see giving themselves to things they shouldn't—all just to find their value and be loved. These are the girls who compromise their self-worth for the attention of boys, who look for relief from life's struggles in drugs and alcohol, or who can't wait to find the next party so they can ignore the problems inside themselves or at home. The problem is that the more they try to hang with others doing these same things, the more they lose their way. God doesn't want you to do this. He doesn't want to lose His girl. He wants you to remain, just as you were from the beginning, completely His.

How do I know? Because God shares His heart for us through His Word—the Bible. And I know it because my dad modeled this care and devotion for me, and he taught me about God's love from an early age. I want you to get to know my dad. He has a lot of wisdom. Sometimes I act like I'm not listening, but I'm actually paying attention. I'll be sharing with you a lot of the life principles I've learned from my dad. I even have a special section that features my dad's advice so you can get it firsthand. I think you'd like him if you met him, and the guy knows what he's talking about. He's the president of the American Association of Christian Counselors and teaches counseling and seminary courses at Liberty University. He has written books and speaks at conferences, colleges, and churches across the country. Most importantly he is a great husband to my mom and a very loving father to Zach and me.

God has also blessed my family with my adopted, older brother, Josh. (Okay, so he's not really adopted, and he's not really my older brother, but he may as well be because he spends so much time with us.) He travels with and works for my dad. He also teaches at Liberty University, writes, and speaks all around the country. Since he came into my life over two and a half years ago, he has been like an older brother to me, offering brotherly advice and looking out for me. Because he's a little closer to our age, I thought it would be a great idea to incorporate some of the life lessons he's taught me along the way. More importantly, he'll help us understand the male perspective a little better. If that's even possible.

So here's a little about me. I'm your average, everyday, small-town girl who wants to know and love God and who cares about people, especially you. My dad is a professional counselor, and I've been lucky to be around him. I've seen how great it is to reach out to others and to get to know them.

I go to an amazing Christian school, but unfortunately dancing is "illegal," and I have to wear the most hideous plaid skirts with tucked-in polo shirts. Maroon, blue, and white are the colors. Talk about a modern-day American flag. Ugh. And double-ugh when a girl would much rather shop at and wear the goods from American Eagle, Nordstrom, Macy's, Hollister, Express, Limited, and Guess. Plaid is not exactly a fashion statement.

Finishing my last year of high school, I'm looking forward to starting college next year. God only knows what I want to be when I grow up. I wish He would tell me.

I love shopping. I love my iPod. I'm a focused student who studies until my brain feels like it is about to fall out. I like to go to the movies, hang out with friends, and go on dates. And yes, I've had my first kiss. By the way, James Blunt's song "You're Beautiful" is sooooooo good! And most of all, I love God.

But honestly, life's not always easy. Both of my grandfathers have passed away, most recently my dad's dad—he was my Papa. One of my best friends was in a coma for over a month after her family was hit by a drunk driver. She now struggles every day trying to relearn everything. Sometimes I ask God why.

I also have minor everyday problems. Boys for instance. For most of my friends, these are more like catastrophes, but you get the picture. I have issues with friends. Bad teachers. And homework every night. I stumble in my walk with Christ just like everybody else does. Doing devotions every day is not always easy.

Such is my journey—my journey with friends, family, love, life, and God. And I consider it a real privilege to invite you along on it. It's a scary thing for me to open up and allow you into my world. But I think that's part of the problem—we fear letting other people in. I really have a hard time trusting others, and I'm not afraid to admit it. For some of you, you have very real reasons not to trust. I have friends who've been hurt deeply by people who were supposed to love them. They especially have a hard time with trust.

I hope that by sharing my experiences, my struggles with life stuff, and the great parts about being a teen ready to face the world, you'll be able to come to trust me. As we journey together through this book, I hope that you'll find more ways that my journey matches your own. That we're asking the same questions. Struggling with the same thoughts. And ultimately trying to be the best we can be for ourselves, our friends, our family, and most importantly, for God.

God loves you. You're His girl. Become totally His.

1

The Real Me

*I want to encourage other people to try to discover who they
are, not to try to fit into some superficial prototype of what they
think a Christian should be, but to discover who they really are.*

—LARRY NORMAN

Have you ever had a frustrating conversation, tried to share how you really felt, and realized nobody got you? Sometimes it's as if the people around you act like they know you, but the reality is that they don't at all! Then when you lie in bed at night, and it's just you and God, do you find yourself praying that somebody—anybody—could see you for who you really are?

Christian singer and songwriter Natalie Grant was bulimic... and has written about it in a song called *The Real Me*. In this song she expresses how God sees the real her, the one hiding behind the skin, hiding behind what other people see. That's a scary thing to think about, that God knows all and sees all. But it's also comforting to believe that God actually knows (and cares about) our deepest desires, longings, concerns, and heartaches. Natalie's honesty has probably helped a lot of girls reach out to God.

Who we are when we are away from others and in the presence of God is who we really are. It's the private inner self. It's the piece we wonder if anybody sees. But the Bible is not silent on this. It says God "sees what is done in secret" (Matthew 6:6). And like I said before, this can be a bit scary, but it can also be a comfort.

Happy with the Life You Already Have

I cannot give you the formula for success, but I can give
you the formula for failure—try to please everybody.
–Herbert Bayard Swope

Mia Thermopolis is a geek. Big glasses. Big, frizzy hair. And can't fit in with the popular crowd. She has a crush on the hottest guy in school—who doesn't even notice she's breathing. So smitten over the popular guy, she herself doesn't even notice the breathing boy who actually has a crush on her—her best friend Lilly's oldest brother, Michael.

If you've watched the movie *Princess Diaries* or read the book by Meg Cabot, you know where the story goes next. Her grandmother comes to town and shocks her with the news that she is born of royalty and is the next heir to the throne. But she has a choice—if she doesn't accept it, somebody else's family will.

Mia decides to take on the new life. From geek to royalty—overnight. She starts taking princess lessons. Straightens her hair. Uses makeup. Hires other people to make her outfits. And she only tells her best friend, Lilly. Nobody else.

But the news spreads. At that point everybody wants to be her friend. Her crush, the popular guy, pursues her. She now has the life she so desired.

Do you know the geek? Maybe you are the geek—or at least you feel like it. You look at everybody else around you, want what they have, and are not satisfied with your life the way it is. Perhaps you cry yourself to sleep at night wishing you had a different life. Wishing you were skinnier. Funnier. Prettier. Smarter. Richer.

Mia did. Then she got it. The looks. The boy. The popularity. And then she realized everybody was out for their own gain. They weren't interested in her. The popular guy liked her for his couple of minutes of fame in the tabloids. He even kissed her. But it was all fake.

In the end Mia discovered that her real friend was Lilly—and her true love was actually Lilly's brother Michael. She learned that the life she wanted to live was really the life she already had—she just didn't know it.

The Search for Significance

No one can make you feel inferior without your consent.
—Eleanor Roosevelt

Isn't it amazing what we'll do to feel like our life matters? To feel important to somebody? To fit in? To discover our place in this world? We go to extremes to be loved. Join the chess club just because Tad joined it. *Maybe he'll notice me,* we think. We spend more money than we should for the latest shoes and clothes. We seek approval from our friends and buy fashion magazines to see what the stars do, say, and wear.

But in our attempts to find the real us, we look in the wrong places and to the wrong people. Have you ever wanted to be like a movie star? I know I have. I buy fashion magazines. I want to look beautiful. I want to be accepted. But where is my limit? Who am I comparing myself to?

Hollywood has presented perfection as a size zero, big boobs, shiny hair, perfect makeup, flawless skin...oh yeah, and did I say *perfect*? Even starlets, who look flawless to us, are constantly criticized. They can't win. They're either too fat or too skinny. There's no limit to the mean comments they receive. There doesn't seem to be a limit to what girls will do to try to be "perfect." Many become anorexic, bulimic, or suffer from severe depression. Yuck! Who wants to be like that? You won't find a star who is on the cover of the tabloids without a problem. But why would we want to be like that? Britney Spears... in the hospital. Lindsay Lohan...in drug rehab. Paris Hilton...in jail. They're searching for their places in the world just as hard as we are.

Why do you think we compare our lives to those of other people so much? Other girls at school, work, and even at church. Think about it for a moment. Who do you secretly compare yourself to? It is usually someone you think, for one reason or another, is better than you. It's normal—I do it too. We compare ourselves to those we see as prettier, skinnier, or more popular than we are. We covet what they have. And where does it get us? Down in the dumps. Anxious. Depressed. And striving for attention. Nowhere.

It's not fruitful. It becomes a vicious cycle of wanting something more or something different than God has given us. I hate to break the news to you, but there's always going to be somebody prettier, skinnier, funnier, smarter, and richer than you are. None of us is perfect.

> *Persons of high self-esteem are not driven to make themselves superior to others; they do not seek to prove their value by measuring themselves against a comparative standard. Their joy is being who they are, not in being better than someone else.*
> —NATHANIEL BRANDEN

During the summer I had severe cystic acne. It was horrible. Every day it felt like it got worse and worse. I hated looking at pictures of girls with perfect skin. I felt so self-conscious. Ever have an experience like that? When you are just sure everyone sees your flaws? Even superstar Hilary Duff said, "I get zits and bad hair just like everyone else. I'm very into embracing your flaws and knowing that you're beautiful for a lot of different reasons."

Other than you, who's expecting you to be a size two? Nobody! You're only putting the pressure on yourself. Ease up. Your significance is not tied to the size of your jeans. And I'm sure that if your photo was digitally touched up the way they do for supermodels, you'd look magazine-cover-ready too. But it's not real! And when you're totally God's, it's all about getting real.

Who Is the Real Me?

Too many people overvalue what they are
not and undervalue what they are.
–MALCOLM S. FORBES

The real me? I'm just your average high school student. The real me gets zits and needs makeup. I have flat hair, small lips, and a weird body (which I'm still trying to figure out). I love my friends. I love my family. I love going to the movies and out on date nights, TP-ing (toilet papering) houses with my friends, playing basketball, and attending school games...pretty much just living my life.

But the real me has fears and worries too. Things I'm afraid to expose.

One night it happened—I was exposed. Unexpectedly. It was one of those nights when I felt gross and grubby. I *didn't* feel like hanging out with my boyfriend or anyone. I was packing my bags because my family and I were leaving for New York City to go Christmas shopping. When the doorbell rang, I thought it was just family dropping by so I rushed downstairs to answer the door. And there he stood! My boyfriend—who decided, just on a whim, to drop by *without* telling me! There I stood. Exposed. No makeup and in my pajamas. This was the first time he had seen me without makeup—*ever.* Can you say *embarrassing*? I thought for sure he was going to take one look at me and want to run away because I didn't look perfect—or close to it. I didn't feel confident. I felt ugly. Every flaw was displayed. Every imperfection revealed. The only people who had ever seen me without my makeup were my girlfriends. And hey, they don't care what I look like and I don't care what I look like in front of them. But I did care what I looked like in front of him. I was scared "the me" beneath the makeup wasn't good enough.

That's when I realized why I have such a hard time exposing the real me. *I'm scared the real me isn't good enough.*

I think it's one of our biggest fears as girls. If I expose the real me—and people find out who I really am—they may not like me. And "me" is everything I have. If you reject that true me, you've rejected everything I have. So instead of facing this possibility, I hide. We hide, don't we?

Sometimes we mask ourselves with our makeup, our clothes, even our school achievements or our friends, because we think these things make us so much more desirable than we really are. We allow our masks to define us. What are you hiding behind?

Our Secret Hiding Places

> *Striving for excellence motivates you; striving*
> *for perfection is demoralizing.*
> –Harriet Braiker

"Eight...nine...ten. Ready or not, here I come!"

We've all played hide-and-seek. If you grow up playing the game in the same house or in the same yard over and over again, you eventually run out of options and begin hiding in the same places. Behind the door. Under the table. In a closet.

I think we do the same in life. We get comfortable with our own secret hiding places. And if every time we play the game they work for us, we keep hiding—until it's what we're known for. Where do we hide? Behind perfectionism. Even under people-pleasing. Let me explain.

Perfectionism

I used to think I had to be perfect 24/7. Everyone seemed to act like I was or that I should be, and I resented the pressure. Some of my friends used to tease me if I made just one mistake, one goof. They acted amazed that I could possibly be at fault. I hated that. I'm not perfect and I never claimed to be.

> *Have no fear of perfection—you'll never reach it.*
> —SALVADOR DALI

I remember when I was about 11, my aunt and uncle came to town. My aunt thought I was this ideal girl. But during their visit, I talked back to my mom, not even disrespectfully but kinda playfully, and my aunt gave me the hardest time about it. It wasn't a huge deal...but I still remember it. I realized then that I didn't want to always be held up as perfect because it was too easy to fall from that pedestal. And too easy to disappoint people.

I do think we try to be perfect in certain areas of our lives. For instance I try to look good all of the time. I don't want to leave the house without makeup. I want to wear nice clothes. I want to keep my weight down and stay physically fit. Those are a few areas of my life I admit I have to be careful I don't hide behind and allow to define me.

Are you a perfectionist? Afraid of getting a B on a test because you're afraid it will hurt your GPA or your reputation for being a perfect student? Is everything in your bedroom organized and arranged just right? Color-coded closet? Books in alphabetical order? Do people know you for being a neat freak? Do these things define you?

Don't get me wrong. I believe good grades and organization are important. But if your behavior gets too obsessive and you become a slave to it or fixated on the reputation you "earn" because of it, it's a sign of a deeper problem. We'll always be let down because the standards we set for ourselves are—in our minds—perfect. When we don't reach them, we're disappointed. When we do reach them, we act like it is no big deal because we expected ourselves to succeed. We never feel rewarded, and we never feel good about ourselves.

Let's stop expecting so much of ourselves. An unreachable expectation is not freedom—it's bondage. If we try to be absolutely perfect in our own lives, we are saying that Jesus' sacrifice on the cross was not enough for us...that there's more to get in life than that. And there's not!

> *A man would do nothing if he waited until he could do it so well that no one could find fault.*
> –JOHN HENRY NEWMAN

People-Pleasing

People-pleasing seems to be built into a lot of girls I know. We love approval. It makes us feel good about who we are. But in our search for significance, we have to learn to base our value on who we are, not on what others think of us.

The tough part is that people-pleasers look great to those around them, especially in the church. They serve everybody. They are the nicest people to be around. And they never seem to be mad at anyone. The pleaser is the girl everybody loves.

But it can be addicting. Hiding behind this mask can make us feel good about ourselves. We think our self-worth, who we are, is found in what others think about us. So we go the extra mile to make sure everybody else around us is okay. Yet inside we're always wondering why we're giving in to the wishes of others, apologizing for things we shouldn't even be sorry about, and saying yes when we should be saying no.

> *I caved in to what people wanted me to do. I thought
> that they weren't going to like me if I didn't.*
> —FIONA APPLE, SINGER

When somebody says, "Megan, you are such a great friend," it strokes my ego a little and makes me want to be a pleaser all the more. But it's the most selfish thing I can do. The only reason we're pleasing other people is to feel good about ourselves. It's a mask. It hides who we really are. We lose our own opinions, likes, and dislikes. And we lose our sense of self in the process. Having a servant's heart is different than being a people-pleaser. When you cross over into people-pleasing, you stop serving God and start serving your own need to be liked or praised.

> *When you please others in hopes of being accepted,
> you lose your self-worth in the process.*
> —DAVE PELZER

Ever see a girl get caught up in pleasing her boyfriend? Giving in to every one of his wishes just so he won't be mad at her or, worse yet, leave her? It's a trap...and she loses her identity in the relationship. You know who I'm talking about. Maybe it's you. If it is, you have to stop giving in and learn to rediscover "the real you."

God created *you* to be just that—*you!* He loves you and wants you to be you.

Your Big Brother's Thoughts on...
The Real You

Megan,

A few months ago I had dinner with Thelma Wells, a well-known speaker and dynamic woman of God. During dinner she asked me, "Josh, what will you be doing in the next five years?"

I had to ponder for a moment because I could tell she was looking for an outside-the-box kind of answer. Then it dawned on me. "Serving Christ," I said.

"Right answer," Miss Thelma replied with a bright beautiful smile.

That made me feel good. But as I drove home that evening, a question popped into my mind as if the Lord was speaking directly to me. "Josh, would you serve Me in five years even if I asked you to change careers—to a position where nobody saw what you did for Me?"

Whoa! Gut check. I must say it scared me a bit. As a guy, I place so much of my identity in what I do. My job. My career. Ask a man who he is and he will tell you what he does. Ask a woman who she is and she'll probably tell you about her relationships. Her relationships with her children, husband, and girlfriends. But we must be careful. Our identity does not lie either in what we do or who we relate with. Our identity is in Christ.

Whether it's your career, husband, boyfriend, children, or even physical appearance, it's easy to place your self-worth or significance in other things—especially if you receive any kind of praise or affirmation for it. Lord knows we all love the attention.

But to be serving Christ wholeheartedly in five years from now, ask yourself this question, "Am I now trying to win the approval of men [others], or of God? Or am I trying to please men [everyone]? If I were still trying to please men [others], I would not be a servant of Christ" (Galatians 1:10).

Live to please God. And you'll discover the real you.

Serving with you,
Josh

Discovering the Real Me

> *I find that the very things that I get criticized for, which is*
> *usually being different and just doing my own thing and just*
> *being original, is the very thing that's making me successful.*
> —SHANIA TWAIN, SINGER

My boyfriend and I had to discuss what we were going to do with our relationship once he left for college. Would we make a commitment? Stay open about other possibilities? We needed to talk. As we spent time praying about it and talking to those we trusted, I jokingly said to one of my friends that we could double-date and have fun as bachelorettes while he was gone. Later that same week, she facebooked my boyfriend behind my back and asked him what he was going to do—basically trying to get the scoop from his perspective. She sent him a message saying that I wasn't going to continue in the relationship once he left because we were on different maturity levels and that he needs to be careful and guard his heart.

I couldn't believe she would do that! She didn't even know what I was feeling! My relationship is *my* business and obviously she is not me. I am not a confrontational person. I avoid confrontation at all cost. But I knew I had to stand up for myself in this moment. No matter how she felt about me after I confronted her, I had to stand up for *me*. I couldn't allow her to tell *my boyfriend* things that weren't true. I talked to my dad about it, and he told me to be true to myself and confront her. So I did. And you know what? I was proud of myself for doing it.

You're a Masterpiece

He [God] molds and shapes each one of us carefully—each
body, mind, and soul—into His exquisite child. We are
beloved and lovable because He is making us that way.

–CHRISTINE GLASS, SINGER

Since that embarrassing episode when my boyfriend unexpectedly showed up on my front steps, he always tells me he loves to see me with my hair all crazy, no makeup on, and my retainer in (gross!). I told him that I didn't believe that...I couldn't believe that. Why would he love that?

He simply responded, "It's you. It's who you are...and I love you!"

Awww. Let me tell you something. It's so nice not having to be perfect. I think that's how God wants us to be too. He wants us to be humble, to need Him, to cry out for Him. God never said we had to be the strong one. He said He would be. God loves your flaws. He loves the real you. The desperate you. The you that needs Him. I don't have to be perfect for God. If I was perfect, I wouldn't need Him. I wouldn't need salvation. I wouldn't need encouragement. But guess what...*I do!*

No matter what I've done or how I've masked the real me, I will always be good enough for God! I haven't earned His love. I'm not perfect. But the fact that He can transform my ugliness, and the mistakes I offer Him into a masterpiece is absolutely breathtaking.

He does the same for you too. He takes you, all of you—the baggage, the tears you cry in the loneliness of the night, even the masks you hide behind—and makes you a masterpiece. Jesus loves you!

What's a Girl To Do?

Use what talents you possess; the woods would be very
silent if no birds sang except those that sang best.

–HENRY VAN DYKE

Do you remember when you were in kindergarten, and you made those clay pots for your mom for Mother's Day? You spent all of your time and energy in art class just on that pot. I remember I painted the outside of my mom's clay pot pink, the inside I painted yellow, and around the top I put a green border. When it came out of the oven, it had cracked. But it was beautiful anyway. I wrapped mine in a brown paper bag—nothing extravagant—and took it home to give it to my mom. It was my best work. I was so excited to give it to her.

What if she would have rejected my gift though? What if she would have said, "Aw, honey, that is nice but it is flawed. I don't want it. I want somebody else's."

When you try to be somebody else and are fearful of being exposed, that's exactly what you're saying to God. You're rejecting the beautiful gift He crafted—you.

When I gave that gift to my mom, she was so excited and grateful. It made me happy, proud that I had made that little pot. I'm almost 18 years old now, and she still keeps her rings in my pink pot. That's how God feels about you! When you offer Him your life—wrapped in a brown paper bag, cracked, pink, green, and yellow—He is so excited. He values you, treasures you, keeps you close to Him, and will always use you if you let Him. What you value the most, God values more. He created you.

Your life matters! You are significant! Your identity is in who God created you to be. Stop trying to be somebody else. Here are a few things to keep in mind:

- *Know that you will fail.* And when you do, learn from it... It's *how* you fail that matters.

- *Surround yourself with people who will help you discover you!* It's like Paula Abdul said: "Everyone is your best friend when you are successful. Make sure that the people that you surround yourself with are also the people that you are not afraid of failing with."

- *Don't overvalue what you're not...and undervalue what you are.* When you beat yourself up, it gets you nowhere. Focus on your strengths! I love what Marcus Aurelius said in *Gladiator:* "I have often wondered how it is everyone loves himself more than the rest of men, but yet sets less value on his own opinions of himself than the opinions of others."

- *Stop trying to be somebody else.* My grandma and I love to sit in the mall and just watch the people who pass by. Have you ever done that? It's amazing. So many shapes and sizes, faces, clothes, colors, smiles, hair (weird hair), and no one person that has passed us has ever looked the same as the next. I love that! I love how creative our God is. I'm so thankful that He made us all unique and different. We were not created to resemble other people... but to resemble Him!

Listening to Dad

- *Your greatest challenge in life will be you.* Don't you allow yourself to believe God doesn't love you or that He doesn't have a plan for you—He does!

- *Be honest with yourself.* Find out your likes and dislikes and focus on your gifts, your strengths, and abilities.

- *Surround yourself with people who will pull you up, not drag you down.* Life is tough enough without having hateful, discouraging people speaking into your life.

- *Know your "blind spots."* Every now and then talk to people who love you about what they see in you. "Faithful are the wounds of a true friend" (Proverbs 27:6 ESV). When people who care for you point out something you need to work on, consider that an act of faithfulness on their end and pay attention.

2

Do You Think I'm Beautiful?

Fashion can be bought. Style one must possess.

–Edna Woolman Chase,
editor in chief of *Vogue* magazine, 1914-1952

Being a girl is awkward. For most girls it seems like one day you roll out of bed and all is good—you're an AA bra size and used to it. The next morning you wake up, start to get dressed, look down, and think, *How did these get there?*

That's how it happened for me. And that's when my mom said, "Honey, we need to go shopping!"

The same thing happened with the curves too. I was always a gangly, knotty, and bony girl, so when I got hips and curves, I had the same reaction, *Whoa, where did these come from?*

I think you know that I'm talking about that most uncomfortable stage of life—junior high. Your body starts changing. Your skin won't cooperate. Your mood changes in an instant. "Happy go lucky" one minute and "don't look at me because I'm mad at the world" the next. As your body changes, so does the way you look and feel about yourself.

I didn't like it when my best friend teased me for the way my body was changing when we hit puberty. I felt very insecure. I felt different. When this happens, you're sure that you're the only one dealing with it. When I told my best friend about how insecure I was, she told me that she had teased me because she was jealous!

We were two middle school girls going through a very natural stage of life, and instead of encouraging one another through it, we were secretly insecure in our own ways about it. She was jealous. I was self-conscious. We were both afraid of being different. Once we realized this, we were able to lift each other up during this weird time.

Every girl experiences it. Even though it is awkward, you will get through it—and you will look fine!

But you can't do it alone.

Today's Beauty

If nature had intended our skeletons to be visible, it would have put them on the outside of our bodies.

–ELMER RICE

In a culture that praises those who are thin and makes fun of those who are overweight, it's no wonder we try to look good. And it seems as though we're never good enough. In a recent *People* magazine, Hilary Duff was quoted as saying, "First I was too fat, then I was too skinny. I realized I couldn't make anyone happy but myself."

- 63% of teen girls feel insecure wearing their swimsuit on the beach.
- 27% think they look hot in their swimsuit.[1]

America seems to have a hard time finding the perfect beauty. Did you know that with digital images and photoshopping, they can change nearly everybody in magazines to look a certain way? Models are getting thinner and more perfect. The more we look at celebrities, the more depressed and guilty we feel about ourselves. If Hilary Duff is having problems figuring out how to look beautiful, I don't stand a chance!

- Most of the models in the magazines are airbrushed— they are not perfect!

- A psychological study in 1995 found that three minutes spent looking at models in a fashion magazine caused 70% of the women to feel depressed, guilty, and shameful.

- Twenty years ago models weighed 8% less than the average woman. Today they weigh 23% less.[2]

What Does It Mean To Be Beautiful?

That which is striking and beautiful is not always good, but that which is good is always beautiful.

–NINON DE L'ENCLOS

I'm sure you've heard someone say, "Inner beauty is all that matters. At least she has a great personality." You know what? I have a problem with that. I recently had a big fat cyst on my face, right next to my nose. It was so embarrassing to wake up every morning to see that thing glaring right back at me in the mirror. Talk about a horn! I was so self-conscious. Have you ever had a major zit on your face or a very bad hair day? Don't tell me it doesn't affect the way you feel about yourself. I'll admit right here and now that the more beautiful and comfortable I feel about my body, the more confident I am. The more confident I am, the better I feel about myself. And others notice! But a girl's gotta find balance. Don't let the physical beauty become your only goal. There is way more to life than external beauty.

Girls going overboard for the fantasy:

- In 2005, 61.7% of American girls were trying to lose weight. 17% of girls had gone without eating for more than

24 hours to avoid gaining weight and/or to lose weight in the last 30 days.[3]

- 50% of teen girls use unhealthy weight control methods such as skipping meals, smoking, purging, taking laxatives, and fasting. Girls who diet are 12 times more likely to binge than girls who do not diet. 81% of 10-year-olds worry they are too fat.[4]

Then there's the reality:

- 95% of those who lose weight gain it all back within 5 years.[5]
- The more a teen diets the more likely she will actually gain more weight in the following three years than if she had not dieted at all.[6]

Inside Out

I remember the girl at school every guy loved to look at. And every girl I knew wanted to look like her. I thought she was beautiful...until I met her.

She was such a perfectionist. Everything had to be just right. Her focus was entirely on herself. But she was also filled with anger, rage, and a drive for perfection. She was a mess on the inside and isolated herself from everybody. Nobody wanted to be around her.

I have since met many girls who, on the outside, are not as radiant as this girl. But their inner beauty draws and endears people to them. What do I mean? Think about the qualities that you love about your best friend. Take a sec and write out a list of these qualities.

I'll never forget when I first met my best friend—we were in third grade, in the choir room. She was the new girl and I asked her if she would be my friend. And it was the best friend-decision I ever made in my life. Believe it or not, we've never been in a fight... which is kind of weird. She is encouraging even when she's not having a good day. She's loyal. I can trust her with anything—and I mean anything—on a very private level. She has great relationships with her family, friends, and her boyfriend. She's funny and I learn from her daily.

Inner beauty makes you even more beautiful on the outside.

	Average Woman	Barbie	Typical Store Maniquin
Height	5' 4"	6' 0"	6' 0"
Weight	145 lbs	101 lbs	Not Available
Dress size	11–14	4	6
Bust	36–37"	39"	34"
Waist	29–31"	19"	23"
Hips	40–42"	33"	34"[7]

Where Inner Beauty Comes From

As I write this chapter, I suddenly realize something—nobody makes me feel more beautiful than my dad. My mom can tell me all day long how beautiful she thinks I am, but it doesn't do the same for me as when my dad says it just once. Not even my boyfriend can tell me I'm beautiful and ignite the same feelings of splendor I get when I hear it from my dad.

I think that whether or not we've been loved and taken care of shows in our beauty. What we have come to believe about ourselves and others shapes how beautiful we appear. I see so many girls trying to *make* themselves be loved in relationships. They work extra hard to be noticed. They compromise their values and beliefs to feel loved. They give in and go further physically. They reveal more about who they are emotionally—more than they ever should or would have—just to feel loved.

If relationships have never been safe for you and you have never felt cherished or beautiful in them, you might go to extremes to find it...to feel it. This is where most girls compromise who they are and what they said they would never do.

Most girls I know have trouble believing that God really loves them. I know that by the way they live. They may say God loves them, but I see them pursue guys. They turn their backs on their girlfriends, give up activities they once enjoyed, and lose their sense of self. All to be noticed. To feel loved. Safe. Beautiful.

When I see this happen, I just want to yell, "Stop! You're trying too hard." So many girls are absolutely beautiful and they just don't know it! Don't get me wrong, I struggle with this too. Let me share with you one of my journal entries from last year.

Journal Entry

Well, today has been kind of a stressful day because of a research problem and a massive zit. I finally shared it with my God. I was challenged to start keeping a journal today! I really want my inner life to affect my outward appearance and experience. Today I want to challenge myself to become more involved with Christ. Too many times I rely on my friends and family to fill the areas only God can. I've been kind of obsessive lately about my appearance. Probably because I would like a boyfriend. How stupid! *My only question to myself is "Why can't I be that obsessive about God?" Look at me...look at how blessed I really am! I am beautiful! God made me unique! From now on, no more obsessing. I want to put my trust and faith completely in God! I surrender! I want to fit God's description: "Many women have done excellently, but you surpass them all. Charm is deceitful, and beauty is vain, but a woman who fears the LORD is to be praised" (Proverbs 31:29-30 ESV). I wish I knew now what God can and will do through me! I hope I am never a distraction or a hindrance toward the plans for my life.*

Don't be desperate. Love will come. I hated when my dad told me that...but it's true. I wanted it to happen immediately! I learned from my dad that I don't have to have "someone." No man can complete me. What I was really looking for no man can give me.

Many of my guy friends have told me that they see right through a girl's attempts to feel beautiful and loved by them. They say it's a huge turnoff. You know what I say? "Girls, let's stop being stupid about it."

When you come to realize this and understand that your beauty is found in God alone, people begin to see you differently. Your beauty is revealed. And when you are beautiful, you are loved and are lovable. There is a freedom about you...not an edge. People draw to you because of your smile. Your freedom.

Your Big Brother's Thoughts on...
A Bridesmaid's Plight

Megan,

I'm sure you've stood at a wedding before and watched the bridesmaids walk down the aisle right before the bride makes her grand entrance. A day when the ladies get all dolled up. A special hair appointment that morning. Manicure and pedicure the day before. Probably even a fake bake in the tanning salon for a few weeks prior. On top of all that is the dress! Think of all that money for one day. And she's not even the center of attention!

But that's not the sad thing. What's sad is when a bridesmaid spends all of that money and effort to look beautiful but forgets to put on a smile! Are you kidding me? From a single guy's perspective, there's nothing worse than a woman who cannot smile. Laugh. And have a good time with life and her relationships. It speaks volumes about her confidence.

Megan, there are a lot of women walking around out there who are either mad at the world, sad about life, or don't believe in their worth. And I'll tell you, it shows. Guys see right through it.

I'll admit, as a single guy, one thing I look for in a woman is her beauty. But it starts from within. It's her countenance that makes her shine. That's the Holy Spirit in her. You can read her depth by the way she carries herself—and it's most evident by the smile she bears. God-fearing women are confident. And confident women smile.

Smile brightly,
Josh

What's a Girl To Do?

You may be asking yourself, "What makes me beautiful?" and "How do I embrace my beauty?"

Here are some things I have learned.

- *God makes you beautiful.* Read Psalm 139 to get a sense of how beautiful God created you to be. He is "enthralled by your beauty" for you are "fearfully and wonderfully made" (Psalm 45:11; 139:14). And "who in the world do you think you are to second-guess God? Do you for one moment suppose any of us knows enough to call God into question? Clay doesn't talk back to the fingers that mold it, saying, 'Why did you shape me like this?' Isn't it obvious that a potter has a perfect right to shape one lump of clay into a vase for holding flowers and another into a pot for cooking beans?" (Romans 9:20-21 MSG).

- *You make you beautiful.* I like what the Greek philosopher Epictetus said, "Know, first, who you are; and then adorn yourself accordingly." If you don't get this piece right, you'll compromise everything. Knowing who you are is so important. You won't be able to set standards and boundaries in your life if you don't know what you like and dislike and what you believe and why you believe it. It's hard to stay true to yourself if you don't know what's true about yourself. When you're confident in what you stand for, others will follow. Find out who you are...then dress yourself up.

- *Others make you beautiful.* Who do you hang out with? Do others speak highly of them? Are they a good influence in your life? Do they make you feel beautiful? Do they encourage you? Love you? Have your best interest in mind? Don't try to be somebody you're not by hanging with a crowd you believe is more popular or better looking or more successful in sports...it will only get you into trouble. Putting it straight—don't hang with hot bodies. Spend time with beautiful souls.

- *Smile more.* Practice smiling. Be a person who is fun to be with. Don't get jammed up about stupid stuff. Be honest with yourself about how you feel and do something about it.

- *Realize God's beauty is different than the world's beauty.* Growing up as a young woman, I know that the world puts so much pressure on you to look a certain way. And the attractive girls win everything...they get all the attention. Or so it seems. But when you really look at others who compromise their lives for meaningless things, you can see by their actions how little they respect themselves. If you want to be beautiful in God's way, respect yourself and who He created you to be.

- *Be classy.* Shania Twain once said, "I don't want my body to be a distraction from my talent or my brain." There's a difference between beautiful and trashy. Be modest and show your style.

- *Get healthy—get active.* I know it's boring and it's tiring. You don't have time. And you rarely see results anyway. If these are your excuses, you are well on your way to living a pretty unhealthy life. Look—exercise disciplines you. If you want to be beautiful and healthy you *must* begin exercising. Not only will it make you feel better and give you more energy throughout the day, but it will also discipline you to eat healthier and maintain your weight. It changes your mindset. And I promise if you stick to it for more than six weeks, you will see results. Start today! You and I can stick with it—I know it.

This reminds me of a funny story I read online about giving up sweets.

> *He was only a chocolate chip cookie...but I loved him.*
>
> I met him at a party. There he was at the end of the buffet.... a loner; the last one on the plate. He had a certain something...a sweetness...he was one hot cookie. I felt as if I'd always known him...hungered for him.
>
> When he looked at me with those warm brown eyes, I melted...With him I could be myself. He didn't seem to care what mood I was in, how I looked or even if I gained weight. Together we had the recipe for happiness. No one satisfied me like Chip.
>
> *Then things changed.*
>
> My friends said he was no good for me. He started to give me heartburn. I felt crummy, but it had to end. Now we've gone our separate ways. I hardly think of him

anymore. Oh, if I see a certain TV commercial, a particular magazine ad, a coupon for money off...that old longing returns. And when we run into each other in the supermarket, we nod. We're friendly. But it's OVER![8]

God's Point of View

*What matters is not your outer appearance—the
styling of your hair, the jewelry you wear, the cut of your
clothes—but your inner disposition. Cultivate inner
beauty, the gentle, gracious kind that God delights in.*
1 PETER 3:3-4 MSG

What God desires is to know that our hearts—our inner souls—are growing to reflect His image more and more every day. That's what He cares about more than anything else—your heart (1 Samuel 16:7).

*Do not lose heart. Though outwardly we are wasting
away, yet inwardly we are being renewed day by day.*
2 CORINTHIANS 4:16 NIV

*The LORD does not look at the things man looks at. Man looks
at the outward appearance, but the LORD looks at the heart.*
1 SAMUEL 16:7 NIV

Search me, O God, and know my heart.
PSALM 139:23 NIV

Above all else, guard your heart, for it is the wellspring of life.
PROVERBS 4:23 NIV

For where your treasure is, there your heart will be also.
MATTHEW 6:21 NIV

But God also wants us to look good on the outside too. The Bible says to "honor God with your body" (1 Corinthians 6:20). We get into trouble, though, when we allow our motives to go beyond what God would desire for our bodies. This is when we begin comparing ourselves to the world's standards. It consumes our thoughts. It becomes the stick we use to measure our self-worth. If you're focusing more on your outer appearance than your heart, mind, and soul, you've lost focus on what beauty is all about. Do you read magazines more than the Bible? My dad always says that you can tell a person's priorities by where they spend their time. Where are you spending yours?

Listening to Dad

- *Respect yourself.* God made you beautiful...just the way He wanted you. If you come to believe that and respect yourself, you'll radiate beauty and confidence.

- *Know who you are.* Knowing who you are is about knowing whose you are. God gave you special gifts, talents, and abilities to use for His glory. When you do, your heart will find fulfillment and joy in who He created you to be.

- *Take care of yourself.* Look and feel beautiful. It builds discipline and character. It all starts within and it shows on the outside. When you strengthen your inner beauty— nourishing your heart, soul, and mind—it will radiate in the way you behave, look, and carry yourself. Always remember, man looks on the outside, but God looks at your heart.

- *Value others.* When you value others, you'll come to respect and value yourself.

- *Be fun to be with.* The sooner you learn to laugh at yourself and about life, the easier life will be for you. Don't take everything so seriously.

- *Talk to someone.* When you are feeling really stuck, knocked down by life, confused, hurt, and not feeling very beautiful, talk to someone about it. Life's too tough to handle by yourself. God is right here for you. Ask Him to direct you toward someone to talk to, to encourage you, and to inspire true beauty in your life.

Cooties or Cuties

Men always want to be a woman's first love—
women like to be a man's last romance.

'll never forget the bedtime stories. Okay...bedtime story. Growing up, my dad read to me every night, sometimes several times a night. He read the same story—*Beauty and the Beast*. It never got old because I joined the story. I became a character.

Did you ever do that? Picture yourself as a character in a story? It always seems like there is at least one person you can relate with. Or one person you want to be.

Me? I wanted to be Belle, the princess. She was smart and she ended up with the prince. I think I tried to live that fairy tale in my own life story as early as kindergarten. I can remember when it was time for our teacher to read to us. I would get so excited on those days because I purposely sat on "the big carpet" next to the boy I liked. He was so cute. I would race to sit right next to him. When we were asked to write a paper on what we were thankful for, I wrote how thankful I was for him.

The very next year I was on homecoming court with a boy named Zachary. He was the first grade cutie. All the girls loved him. And I was the one who got to walk with him at homecoming. I was so excited. Then I found out that my best friend liked him—so I didn't like him anymore.

After that I don't remember being too interested in boys. My girlfriends mattered more. Boys were—well, they were just that—boys. I didn't understand them. Still don't today, but...

Something changed. The boys started paying attention to me and my friends.

Pretty soon they became the focus of our conversations. In the cafeteria, in the classroom, after school, at church...our conversations went from dolls, tea parties, and cooties to tree houses, friends, and cuties. Truth is, no matter where we are, it's all about boys. Whether it's algebra, trigonometry, calculus, physics, or geometry, they are the theorem we are trying to prove. In science class, boys are the creatures we are dissecting. In English lit, the story we are trying to unfold. Admit it, girls...you have said these words, "He's so cute."

What is a good age to start dating?

Parents' views:

Age:	% of parents
12	9%
13	8%
14	12%
15	16%
16+	42%
No set rule	10% [1]

The questions we ask: Does he think I'm cute? How do I know if he's interested in me? He told me he would call, but why haven't I heard my new ring tone I set for him? Why hasn't he sent me a text? If he likes me so much, why hasn't he asked me out yet?

In our attempt to console our heartbroken girlfriends with compassionate but superficial answers, we secretly wonder ourselves if we truly believe our own advice.

Remember in the introduction when I said I love the song *You're Beautiful* by James Blunt? Yeah, well...doesn't it seem like that's what we all long to hear? That some guy somewhere really thinks we're beautiful, and that he admires us even from afar. Deep down we wonder if we'll ever get the man who thinks we're beautiful.

What's Going On?

Don't marry the person you think you can live with; marry only the individual you think you can't live without.
–Dr. James C. Dobson

Text messaging until two in the morning, waiting for the phone to ring, even interpreting his text messages to figure out what the dot-dot-dot means versus the smiley face, it is easy to become consumed with trying to read into what a boy really means by the messages he sends. Is he into me or not? Why do we drive ourselves crazy?

Because we want to be loved!

There is something about having somebody like us that makes us feel good. My little eleven-year-old brother, Zach, came home the other day pumped that the cute girl with the locker next to his likes him. When you feel liked or loved, it makes you feel special... crazy inside.

I remember the first time a boy I liked told me I was beautiful. My brain became scrambled eggs. I couldn't think. It made me crazy.

Your heart races. You almost feel out of control, not sure what to say back or what to do next. Do you hug him? Tell him he's beautiful too? No, wait, that's unmanly. I may offend him.

I hope you're beginning to understand what I'm talking about. When you catch that glance and lock eyes, it suddenly dawns on you that somebody just might be interested in you.

Reading Him Like a Book

You don't love a woman because she is beautiful;
she is beautiful because you love her.
–Author Unknown

Picture this. A new boy just moved in three houses down the street from where you live. You've watched him help his dad around the house for about two weeks prior to the start of school. You know he is cute and he's about your same age. When the first day of school arrives, he is sitting only two seats away from you in homeroom. All of the girls are talking about him. During the first week of school, he somehow finds out you live in the same neighborhood. By Friday he asks you to help him get used to his new surroundings. Score! He noticed!

So on a warm September Saturday morning you go for a walk around your neighborhood. You are really hitting it off. You find out he played in a Christian band where he used to live. His dad is a pastor. He seems genuine. Sweet. Nice. Caring. Along the course of your walk, he points to the most beautiful house in the neighborhood saying, "Wow, that house is beautiful!"

Stop...

What goes through your mind? You have a really sweet, nice, caring, genuine boy, who is totally hot I might add, walking with you on a beautiful September morning and he says, "Wow, that house is beautiful!" Admit it...you're thinking, *He totally pictures me in that house with him one day!*

From then on, you read into every move he makes, becoming more and more excited because these are sure signs he likes you. All the while you totally discount the clear signs that he doesn't! Our minds take our hearts to places they should not go. And we become confused.

Does he like me? Why doesn't he just ask me out? My friends think he likes me. He treats me differently than other girls. Blah...Blah...Blah. We get consumed. And the next thing we know, he is all we think about.

> Dear Megan,
>
> Sometimes I think you just need to go for it. If you really, really like him and you don't think it's just going to be one of those two-week relationships, I believe it's okay to just go for it. I mean, there is this guy I've known for about four months now. We have hung out in groups and spent a lot of time together recently, going to basketball games and other school events. He is a great Christian guy and has a wonderful family. I am sure he likes me. LOL. Is there anything wrong with asking him out?
>
> Thanks for your help,
> Anxious Annie, age 16

Dear Anxious Annie,

You can definitely not ask him out. Are you desperate or what? Sorry, didn't mean to sound rude. I just don't want you to settle. If he is not asking you out, it's because of one of two reasons. 1) Either he's afraid of making important decisions and going after what he wants, or 2) he's just not into you. If it's the first one, look out. I am not so sure of his ability to make important decisions in life and stand by them. If it's the second one, you don't want him. Either way, if he's stuck and can't decide, something else is going on.

Besides, don't rush it. You've only known the boy for four months. Based on the 79.6 years a girl is expected to live, four months is less than one half of a percent of your life! If you are enjoying one another's company in group settings, continue doing so.

Remember this. Solomon said, "There is a proper time

and procedure for every matter, though a [woman's] misery weighs heavily upon [her]" (Ecclesiastes 8:6). Make sure to seek God's guidance in the proper time and procedure for all matters, even in relationships with boys!

Your friend,

Megan

What You Deserve

> *Boys are beyond the range of anybody's sure understanding, at least when they are between the ages of 18 months and 90 years.*
> —JAMES THURBER

Aren't we all like Anxious Annie? You see a cute boy. He appears "godly." Everybody likes him. He's involved at school. Volunteers at church. And of course, he treats you differently than he does the other girls! Or so you like to think...

And in some hormonal state of anxiety you think that if you don't snatch him up now, the rapture may beat you to it. Or worse yet, another girl! Anxiety sets in. You check his Facebook every opportunity you have. Did somebody post something? You must act. Now!

So we do. We go to all sorts of extremes trying to impress the boy we are certain God spent so much time designing specifically to be our personal knight in shining armor. We relate to him in ways we best know how. We dress up. We are on our best behavior. We try to be friendly. And we manipulate our way into his life. (Yes, whether we admit it or not, we are great manipulators.)

Girls' Attitudes Toward Boys

- Anxious Annie: "I've just got to have him."
- Hungry-for-Attention Hannah: "Since he talked to me, he must totally be into me."

- M.R.S. Mary: "If I'm not married by 21, there is something wrong with me."
- Physical Phyllis: "If I give in to what he wants physically, I'm sure he'll love me forever."
- Friendly Faith: "We have been friends for so long now; God wants us to be together."
- Prayerful Pattie: "God told me that boy was the one I would marry."
- Savior Sue: "He isn't a Christian, but I just know that if I date him he will get saved."

Our actions are born out of our attitudes. You've heard it said, "Your attitude, not your aptitude, determines your altitude." Unfortunately it's true. Your attitude toward life, including boys, will determine your altitude, or success, in the future. If I think I must have him now, I will more than likely compromise the long lasting relational qualities I am looking for in a boy in exchange for a temporary fix of having him by my side. Take Anxious Annie for instance. In her attempt to have the boy she is ever so certain likes her, she will trade off what her heart desires for the comfort of having him in her life now!

I know it's tough if all of your friends have boyfriends and you don't! It can get lonely. You are the third wheel. Or the fifth wheel. Tagging along in groups of couples. Alone. Not feeling cuddled. Not being chased. Left wondering, *What's wrong with me?*

Look around you. How many of your friends were actually chased? Did the boys they are with now really pursue them like they were princesses? Not just any princess, but the only princess in the universe. It's what you deserve.

Made for Relationship

Keep vigilant watch over your heart; that's where life starts.
PROVERBS 4:23 MSG

So the question you are probably asking is "Why *am I* so focused on boys?" What is really behind the rush we believe we're in—this anxious state of emergency causing us to act now or lose out on the proverbial "man of my dreams"?

Please understand that I am not writing this to make you feel guilty. I don't want to be another voice in your life telling you that "if you focus totally on God, you won't think of boys at all." Truth is you may have been taught that all you need is God and an over-emphasis on boys is unhealthy and reflective of a poor spiritual life. As a result you may feel shameful and guilty for even having feelings for a boy.

Remember that Adam was in perfect union with God in the Garden of Eden. He was sinless. Nothing hindered his relationship with God. And yet, something still wasn't good! "It's not good for the Man to be alone; I'll make him a helper, a companion" (Genesis 2:18 MSG).

We were created for relationship, to be in union with one another, just as God the Father, the Son, and the Holy Spirit are in union with one another in the Godhead. Having a boyfriend is not necessarily the problem. You are not "unspiritual" if you are interested in boys. The problem comes when we get too consumed by our interest in boys.

Why We Chase

The real secret to total gorgeousness is to believe in yourself, have self confidence, and try to be secure in your decisions and thoughts.
–KIRSTEN DUNST

What does it mean to approach boys in a godly way? To give part of who we are to a boy, yet remain totally His? Totally God's?

First, recognize your desire to be loved. To feel safe. To be wanted. After polling my friends, 100 percent of them said they want to be loved. It's natural!

Unfortunately the compulsion or desire to seek boys and be loved comes from the fall of mankind. "And you will desire to control your husband" (Genesis 3:16 NLT). In this passage God's curse on woman is that we desire control, particularly in relationships. When we're in control, life feels safe. This verse doesn't necessarily refer just to husbands. If it did, most of you would tune me out. What girls want in relationships is protection. We want to feel safe. We want to be wanted.

When we see something *we think* we need, we go after it. Boys are no exception. They are probably the most sought after item of any female. When we see the boy we think we cannot live without, we do our best to get him to notice us. Remember when I said earlier we are great manipulators?

We want to be noticed. Wanted. Chased.

But you cannot manipulate. You cannot make somebody love you.

Journal Entry

I haven't journaled in a while...I'm actually sorry about that. Last weekend was amazing! But tonight that's not where my heart is. I feel the separation again! Why are things wonderful one weekend and then horrible the next? Why? I can't make him love me even though I could cry out my eyes and hand him my heart! I know, Lord, that I am unhappy because I have tried to fill Your place in my heart with my boyfriend! I feel like a rubber band that is being stretched to the farthest possible limits and is about ready to break! I'm scared he doesn't love me anymore. I'm scared he likes someone else—someone better! He tells me he loves me and kisses me softly...I just need to hear him and look at him and have him say "I love you" like he did the first time.

Lord, here is my relationship, imperfect and scary, but beautiful and unique. Thank You, Lord, that You know my heart and my boyfriend's heart. Father, push me or pull me away—I have to know. Guide and protect my fragile heart! It's weak tonight. Fill my spirit with Your unspeakable joy! I pray in Jesus' name. Amen.

The Cry of Our Hearts

Most Christians will tell you that it's not appropriate for girls to pursue boys. And I hope you are beginning to understand why. It's not your job. Remember, you were not designed to chase. You were designed to be chased.

But here's where manipulating comes in. We put ourselves in positions where we can be near him. We find ways to be in his study group. His Bible study. His youth group. We may set up a "date" whereby "the girls" end up not-so-accidentally running into "the boys" at the mall. All in an attempt to get the boy to what? Notice us!

Be careful though. Many times in your attempt to get him to notice you, you become the chaser...not the chased! And when you chase, it usually equals disaster.

My "older brother," Josh, tells me that warriors (guys) come in many different personalities and packages so be sure to pay close attention to who the guy really is and what he stands for. You might be surprised at who your warrior might be!

If the guy hasn't asked you out, if he's stuck and undecided, something else is going on and it's time for you to move on. If you're already in the relationship and you sense his lack of care or attention, and yet you stick around because you don't want to be alone or because you want to stay devoted no matter what, then you're probably loving too much. This can get us girls into trouble.

Girls Who Love Too Much

The best way to mend a broken heart is time and girlfriends.
–GWYNETH PALTROW

My dad and I were talking about this the other day, and he said that girls who did not have a good dad or positive male figure in their lives typically find boys similar to what they saw around them. They find cheaters. Players. Narcissists (that's a word my dad uses for boys who are stuck on themselves). Some are even abusers. And yet girls run back to these annoying guys who believe they are God's gift to women. Girls sacrifice their own dreams to run after something less than God's ultimate best!

What about the girl who cannot live without a boy? She goes from relationship to relationship—boyfriend to boyfriend—each time believing she has found "the one." She says nothing bad about him, kisses the dirty ground he walks on, and, oh yeah, becomes a space cadet. Two months later he starts dating one of her friends and becomes not just a jerk but a jerk with a capital J.

Then, just when you think she is going to... No, wait. Oh no, she didn't? Oh yes she did. One week later there's another guy. And she says he's...*wonderful!* You see the cycle? She gets hurt. Again.

Girls Hurt by Boys

For many of these girls, boys are evil. A girl I know recently joined a group on Facebook.com called "If It Weren't for Guys...Girls' Lives Would Be Perfect." The description: "This group is created for girls who would have the perfect, problem-free life if it weren't for the opposite sex." It seems the woman who once said, "If they could put one man on the moon, why can't they put them all?" may now have a fan base. On the surface it appears these girls and countless others have a hard time coexisting *with* the male species.

Haters

I know some girls who say they just downright hate boys mostly because they've been hurt by them. Sometimes this hurt is so deep it's as though the hate becomes a sort of protection. They protect themselves from boys because they've learned that boys can hurt them or let them down. My dad said this can happen when a significant male role model (typically the father) betrayed their trust early on.

On the other hand, I have yet to meet a girl so miserable that she ultimately decided to ditch boys altogether. I wonder if the reason we can't live with or without boys is because we can't figure them out. Or maybe we're looking in the wrong places for the answers. Or... maybe the problem is that we're looking, that we're more focused on *them* than we are on God and our relationship with Him.

Your Big Brother's Thoughts on...
Swimming Safe

Megan,

One of the problems you'll face in the dating world is the difference between how boys and girls view relationships. For instance, when you define the relationship as friends, boys see you as that, just a friend. When both of you have defined it as boyfriend/girlfriend, boys see you as that, a girlfriend. They compartmentalize. Separate. Think of a swimming a pool. To separate the deep end from the shallow end, a rope with buoys is placed across the pool from one side to the other. Boys see a deep end and they see a shallow end. They see you as a friend. Or they see you as a girlfriend. It's up to them to put the rope across the pool. When they do...they'll tell you.

The problem with this is that girls, on the other hand, see the entire swimming pool! Even when the rope is connected, you still see what? A pool. It's the same with relationships. Where guys see you strictly as a friend, you see relationship. Where guys see you strictly as a girlfriend, you see relationship. What guys separate, girls mix. And it's here where girls and guys fail to figure one another out!

He may lavish you with gifts. Treat you like a queen. But if the relationship is defined strictly as friends, he still sees you as that...a friend! Don't fall into the trap of being pursued by a boy who, after a reasonable period of time, doesn't redefine the relationship as boyfriend/girlfriend. If you feel your heart moving his direction, beware! You deserve to be chased by someone who will protect your heart. Don't waste your time on a boy playing games with it.

If he is really that into you, he will make it known!

With concern,
Your Big Bro

- 60% of those teens who marry before age 18 divorce within 15 years.
- 50% of those age 18-19 who marry divorce within 15 years.
- 30% of those over 20 divorce within 15 years.[2]

What's a Girl To Do?

How we look at and approach boys will impact the quality of relationships we have with them in the future. Spending time with boys who treat you the way you want to be treated encourages you to set your standards high. But you probably won't hang with boys of this caliber if you're not spending time with God.

> *Girls are like apples...the best ones are at the top of the trees. The boys don't want to reach for the good ones because they are afraid of falling and getting hurt. Instead, they just get the rotten apples that are on the ground that aren't as good, but easy. So the apples at the top think there is something wrong with them, when, in reality, they are amazing. They just have to wait for the right boy to come along, the one who's brave enough to climb all the way to the top of the tree.*
>
> –AUTHOR UNKNOWN

I hate to admit this, but it really is true. My relationships with boys start with my relationship with God. It's the same for all of us—we are His first! He created us. His longing and prayer is to be with you—"Father, I want those you gave me to be with me, right where I am" (John 17:24 MSG).

He is watching you.

> And if God gives such attention to the appearance of wildflowers—most of which are never even seen—don't you think he'll attend to you, take pride in you, do his best for you? What I'm trying to do here is to get you to relax, to not be so preoccupied with getting, so you can respond to God's giving. People who don't know God and the way he works fuss over these things, but you know God and how he works. Steep your life in God-reality, God-initiative, God-provisions. Don't worry about missing out. You'll find all your everyday human concerns will be met.
>
> Give your entire attention to what God is doing right

now, and don't get worked up about what may or may not happen tomorrow. God will help you deal with whatever hard things come up when the time comes.

Matthew 6:30-34 MSG

Even though you can't always see it, you are "squinting in a fog, peering through a mist. But it won't be long before the weather clears and the sun shines bright! [You'll] see it all then, see it all as clearly as God sees [you], knowing him directly just as he knows [you]" (1 Corinthians 13:12 MSG). God really does love you. He really does have your best interest in mind.

We represent Christ in all of our being and all of our actions—in the car on Friday night, in every text message we send, in every lunch conversation we hold, in every game we play, in every relationship we have—in everything.

As you live for God and seek to be loved by Him remember:

- You are beautiful in God's eyes.
- God created you with a desire to be loved.
- God loves you.
- God chases you.

Having relationship difficulties? Remember:

- *Don't chase guys.* Your heart is worth fighting for! Don't compromise it by pursuing guys when you should wait and be patient for a warrior to pursue you.

- *Rebound relationships never work and relationships won't fix you.* If you can't remember when you've been without a boyfriend, you may need to be single for a while.

- *Go slow.* You might want an instant relationship, but you can't force a good thing. As your parents decide when you can date, be willing to wait for this time. And then be willing to wait until there is a good, godly guy who captures your interest. *You* are worth the wait and your happiness is worth waiting for.

- *Use a spiritual barometer.* Does he have a genuine relationship with God? Would he encourage you in your faith and your standards? Don't just measure a guy by his looks, his clothes, or his sweet talk. Measure him by his God talk.

- *Begin praying every night for the man God will bring into your life.*

As King David declares, "Stay with GOD! Take heart. Don't quit. I'll say it again: Stay with GOD" (Psalm 27:14 MSG). And when you do, your love for God, life, and boys (or should I say *men*) will never die but be made complete. Because perfect love has no fear!

Listening to Dad

- *Know how serious this is.* Have fun being friends with boys. But when it starts getting serious with one, know this... the most important decision you will make in life, apart from committing your heart and faith to Jesus, is the decision of who you will marry. Choose wisely.

- *Be patient.* Don't try to fill the hole in your heart with a boy. Only your heavenly Father can fill that void.

- *Never compromise your values.* Make a list of at least five standards and stick to them. Never compromise who you are for a boy.

- *Be sure there is magic between you and the boy you are with.* You should feel tingly. Warm. Loved. Now remember, it won't always feel tingly. You will have difficult times. But more than not, you deserve to be giddy. Love is beautiful. It should feel that way too.

- *Make sure he respects you.* He should never put you in a position where your values are challenged or compromised. He should be your protector.

- *Find out how he treats his mom and other women in his life.* This is a good indicator. By doing this you'll learn if he is kind, generous, helpful, and respectful.

> *Husbands, go all out in your love for your wives, exactly as Christ did for the church—a love marked by giving, not getting. Christ's love makes the church whole. His words evoke her beauty. Everything he does and says is designed to bring the best out of her, dressing her in dazzling white silk, radiant with holiness. And that is how husbands ought to love their wives. They're really doing themselves a favor—since they're already "one" in marriage.*
> Ephesians 5:25-28 msg

4

Sex and Sexy

*For a kiss to be really good, you want it to mean something...You
can't cheat your first kiss. Trust me, you don't want to. Cause
when you find that right person for a first kiss, it's everything.*
—ALEX KAREV, CHARACTER FROM *GREY'S ANATOMY*

Every girl dreams of that perfect kiss. You know what I'm talking about...the one you see in every movie and read about in every magazine. Remember Mia in *Princess Diaries?* She always wanted her foot to "pop." By the end of the movie, she got that foot-poppin' kiss.

So did I...

Journal Entry

*Today has been one of the greatest nights of my life! Not only did I
go to a really fun birthday party, but...I got my first kiss!!! Ahhh!
Talk about "can you feel the love tonight!" LOL. So he drops me
off at my house and we are waiting outside when he unexpectedly
kisses me! I mean, yeah, I was kinda expecting and hoping, but yet
I wasn't sure if he would. It was an awkward yet amazing experience. I am like in another world! The first two were just like pecks,
but then as he goes to leave, he gives me that smile...you know
what I mean. It was freezing tonight so I was wearing these super
cute fluffy turtle socks from Aéropostale. Being the weirdo I am,
I showed them to him, and he said they were the best part of his
night! I knew he was just teasing me...so I gave him that "look,"*

and he starts hobbling along (crutches) and then says, "Come and prove me wrong!" So I did. I followed him to his car and smiled and said, "Yes," so we kissed again for longer than a second! Ahhh! I'm head over heels! Sweet dreams!

We all dream about that passionate moment when the world seems to stop for us, even if it's just for a second. Kissing does something to us...it touches our hearts and that's the way God designed it.

When I was little, I used to have a fabulous collection of Barbie dolls. I loved playing with them, dressing them up, and making Barbie beautiful for Ken. He was a hottie. I couldn't wait for them to get married. I would dress Barbie in the most elaborate, beautiful wedding gown I could find. After the preacher (who was usually a G.I. Joe from my brother's collection) performed the ceremony, Ken and Barbie would kiss. The kiss was innocent, pure, and really beautiful.

When we're young, simple things like kisses are beautiful and pure. Yet as we mature we wonder why we have taken such a simple, pure thing like kissing and stripped it of its innocence.

> The longest kiss listed in the *Guinness World Records* lasted an incredible 417 hours. (Wow, that's one insanely long smacker!)

Did You Say *Sexy*?

We don't have to find love and acceptance and escape through doing drugs and alcohol and engaging in promiscuous sex. When they see us not only talking about God but living our faith 24/7, that's our loudest witness about what real "love" looks like.
—Rebecca St. James

Let me just say it outright. I want to be sexy! Yeah, I said it! But I have to ask, what is "sexy"? Is it trashy? Or can it be beautiful?

The media would have us believe sexy is something altogether different. They push us to believe that who we are is defined by what we look like, how little we wear, or how likely we are to get the "hot guy" to "hook up" with us. Have you noticed the pressure to be flirtatious and even trashy? Watch MTV or VH1 and you get pounded by images and statements declaring that real love is found by accepting statements like "any attention is good attention" and "if you really love me, you'll have sex with me." These presentations glamorize destructive attitudes; they don't lift up true love. I often wonder if it's really that satisfying for any of those people.

I have never been asked to have sex, do drugs, or smoke. People know what I stand for. It's who I am. I am so thankful that I have never been placed in a tempting situation like that. My boyfriend has never made me uncomfortable—but then again, I refuse to date someone who would take advantage of me. You too should make that vow. My parents always taught me to respect myself and my body. Why? This body is not mine, it's God's!

> There is a sense in which sexual sins are different from all others. In sexual sin we violate the sacredness of our own bodies, these bodies that were made for God-given and God-modeled love, for "becoming one" with another. Or didn't you realize that your body is a sacred place, the place of the Holy Spirit? Don't you see that you can't live however you please, squandering what God paid such a high price for? The physical part of you is not some piece of property belonging to the spiritual part of you. God owns the whole works. So let people see God in and through your body (1 Corinthians 6:18-20 MSG).

Did you read that? *All* of you is owned by God. I think there is a distinct difference in being sexy and trashy. Sexy is confidence, beauty, and—listen to this—full coverage of all your body parts. Your body is God's temple.

Sexy is also a state of mind. It's who you are when you are just being *you!* And that's what this chapter's about—being sexy by just being *you!*

In Pursuit of Sexy

> *The truth is…a guy would much rather play a challenging game of basketball than an easy game of Candy Land. Make the pursuit of you more difficult and watch him melt at your feet!*
> —HAYLEY DIMARCO

On almost every cover of any women's magazine you'll find headings like, "How to Get Sexy Fast," or "Ten New Ways to Feel Sexy." You might dig through the pages just to find the tips. In a recent *People* magazine, 45 percent of women said heels make them feel sexy the instant they put them on. Isn't it really easy to put something on that makes you feel sexy? Today, in almost every store you go in, you can find at least one miniskirt and a super-low-cut shirt…even in winter! I always want to look good, but when "good" compromises who I am, I have a problem with that.

So does Hayley DiMarco who is the author of *Sexy Girls*. I love what she says: "If it ain't on the menu, keep it covered up!" In Rebecca St. James' book, Rebecca wrote that your bathing suit covers up parts of your body for a reason. Whatever it covers up is meant to be covered up. Or as a youth pastor once said, "Maybe your purity pledge should start to include where you shop!"

In your pursuit of sexy, know what God thinks is sexy. "Looks aren't everything. Don't be impressed with…looks and stature… GOD judges persons differently than humans do. Men and women look at the face; GOD looks into the heart" (1 Samuel 16:7 MSG). I believe that sexy begins with our relationship with God. When we purify our hearts and seek to be set apart for God, we become more and more beautiful on the outside. Without the cleavage.

Hanging Out, Hooking Up, and Friends with Benefits

Okay, so we all know the terms. Hooking up. Making out. Friends with benefits. But what does it all mean? It seems like most of the culture, including many Christians, have gone from dating... to just getting physical. Everyone wants to think they can have their cake and eat it too. The benefits without the commitment. It's as if we believe we can get physical yet keep our distance so that if the relationship ends, we won't hurt as much. But it doesn't really work that way. Ask any girl whose heart has been broken over and over when sex or sexual behavior didn't lead to anything except a reputation and a lot of tears.

> *Why does a man take it for granted that a girl who flirts*
> *with him wants him to kiss her—when, nine times*
> *out of ten, she only wants him to want to kiss her?*
> –Helen Rowland

We all know kids at school who "get around." They do "it" all the time. Everyone knows it and everyone keeps quiet. I have never been one of those girls. I have no desire to have sex. Is the temptation there? Sure. But if I gave in, I would feel so cheap. My heart and my body are reserved for one person—my husband.

Let me restate 1 Corinthians 6:19 (MSG) again, "Didn't you realize that your body is a sacred place, the place of the Holy Spirit? Don't you see that you can't live however you please, squandering what God paid such a high price for?" When we live to please ourselves and feel good in the moment, we squander not only our own bodies, but those of the ones we "hook up" with. If there is no commitment, there should be no sexual touching. To me it's that simple. Look again at what Paul wrote, "So let people see God in and through your body" (1 Corinthians 6:20 MSG). Is what you're doing through your body with your boyfriend, random guys, or your friends radiating God?

- 68% of teens think they have been in love, 12% have not ever been in love, and 18% thought they were in love, but realized it turned out to be something else.[1]
- 52% of teens believe they know the difference between love and lust, 28% are not sure.[2]

I like to think of it this way. Would you be doing the same things if you saw Jesus sitting beside you right now? Would you be embarrassed? Better yet...what if the person you are going to marry is doing the same thing you are doing right now with somebody else?

Tough questions. But we all need to ask them.

Believing in and Understanding Purity

A good time is a pleasure which has no aftermath of regret.
–ANONYMOUS

On my fourteenth birthday, my family took me out to dinner at the Chop House. We had a great time just enjoying each other's company. Before the night was over, my dad gave me a present. It was in a small box, and I couldn't wait to open it. I unwrapped the gift and looked inside. There it was—a beautiful diamond ring, a purity ring.

That day I made a promise to my dad that I was going to remain pure for my husband and him only. I wear that ring every day...so when I am in a tempting situation, I can look down at my ring and say, "No, I can't do this. I promised my dad I wouldn't." Someday I'm going to be able to point to that ring and say to my husband, "I saved myself for you. I'm completely yours, mentally and physically, forever!"

Why won't I have sex? I want to respect my dad and mom. I want to respect my future husband. And most importantly, I want to respect God. If you haven't committed yourself to a life of purity, then I suggest you do that. Buy your own purity ring if you have to. Most girls I know do. Then pray to God and commit your body to Him. If you need help, use the prayer in the journal entry as a guide. God will listen and help you in times of temptation...but only if you seek Him daily.

> *What's honest is this: Chastity is God's very best for us. God*
> *created sex for marriage and that is where it belongs.*
> –LAUREN WINNER, FROM HER BOOK *REAL SEX*

Journal Entry

This verse has challenged me today. "Didn't you realize that your body is a sacred place, the place of the Holy Spirit? Don't you see that you can't live however you please, squandering what God paid such a high price for? The physical part of you is not some piece of property belonging to the spiritual part of you. God owns the whole works. So let people see God in and through your body" (1 Corinthians 6:19-20 MSG). *I'm not perfect! But I am God's design and His daughter.*

Lord, today I am making a commitment to You. Use this body because it is Yours! I am sinful and helpless, but through You I am untouchable and amazing and most of all...beautiful! Speak to me and tell me Your plans. Teach me how to have a closer relationship with You. Forgive me for falling short in my relationships. Help me to overcome any temptations and live a pure life for You, Father. I love You so much and long to serve You! You are holy! Forgive me for not living up to my fullest potential for You! Guide me now and forever.

Love,
Megan

How Far Is Too Far?

I have always been taught about sex like this: Your body is a gift—a beautiful gift—and on it is a name tag with the name of one man. If you let other guys touch your body and be rough with it, they will damage it and damage you. On your wedding night do you want to present your husband with a gift half opened, or worse, torn open and already used?

Honestly speaking, you know what is too far for you. I don't think kissing is wrong. I enjoy kissing! It's a fun way to express love. Some people need the physical touch—like holding hands. It may be how you express love. It's your love language. You just have to be careful and learn where your boundaries lie. For instance, my boyfriend will not come into my room unless there is an adult close by or in the room with us. We also try to do things with my family and set up double dates with friends. But you do have to realize that someone is not always going to be with you. So boundaries are very important to establish and hold on to.

In a study on adolescents' beliefs about virginity and abstinence:

- 83.5% thought they were still a virgin after genital touching.
- 70.6% considered themselves a virgin after oral sex.[3]

There are some shocking statistics about what teens believe about what does or doesn't count as sex. All I have to say is *sex is sex*...no matter how it is performed! That's why it's important for us to set boundaries and to respect and care about our bodies as much as God does. If a girl redefines sex just to make herself feel better about going further than planned, she is only cheating herself and compromising the future relationship God wants for her.

What If I've Already Slipped Up?

You cannot make yourself feel something you do not feel, but you can make yourself do right in spite of your feelings.

–PEARL S. BUCK

Statistics show that a lot of you have already gone too far. But you know what? God is so awesome. He is waiting for you to confess and come clean before Him. If you have slipped up and given yourself over to lust rather than hold out for love and God's best for you and your future, you can give your mistakes over to Him. Do that. And begin, from this day forward, to be chaste—clean until your honeymoon! You won't regret it.

- 30% of those who have sex wish they had waited
- 8% wish it had been different[4]

Your Big Brother's Thoughts on...
Being Sexy

Megan,

Want a godly guy? I don't know a Christian girl who doesn't.

What are godly guys looking for in a girl? First, if you say you believe in God, live it. Guys don't want to hear all of your Christian jargon and then watch you live life just like every other girl out there. It's not sexy. When it comes to what you believe and who you are, your actions speak louder than your words. Let your actions do the talking.

Secondly, it is a huge turnoff to a guy when a girl is needy. Don't pursue him or even make it look like you are. A godly guy wants a girl made so complete by her love relationship with God that though she may allow her boyfriend to take care of her, she doesn't need him to. And finally, respect yourself...and be mysterious. The more you flaunt yourself physically and emotionally, the less mysterious you are—meaning the less interesting you are to him. Respect yourself and keep him guessing. He wants to fight for you. Make him.

Stay sexy,
Josh

What's a Girl To Do?

It's a difficult area to deal with. If you struggle with going too far physically, you may have to set stricter boundaries. Following some of these guidelines will help you resist temptation.

- *Respect yourself...respect him.* This is where it starts. Respecting your body and his body as God's property reduces the chance of going too far.

- *Don't kiss lying down.* It is too easy to move from passionate kissing to other things you don't want to do.

- *It's okay to snuggle, but...*Don't lie on top of one another and certainly don't snuggle while lying down.

- *Don't touch or be touched there.* You know where I mean.

- *Keep yourself out of compromising situations.* Don't go places where you have too much freedom. Make sure there are people nearby. Physical touch is a powerful and appealing way to express how we feel...God made it that way, and because of that, God wants us to set boundaries. The Bible says not to burn with passion. It is easier to compromise faster here than in any other area of my life. So protect yourself by staying away from tempting situations that lead to compromise and mistakes.

- *If you've already messed up, confess and recommit.* A great song by Sara Evans called "Always Be My Baby" is a confession of going too far physically. It reflects how any of us would feel—afraid that God would be angry and that He would leave us. But as the song reveals, instead of blasting us with anger, God showers us with His love. Check out that song sometime. It's powerful and it's real because God tells each and every one of us that we will always be His baby—no matter what.

  I'm so thankful that we serve a loving and forgiving God who gives us second chances. That doesn't mean we might not suffer from the consequences of our choices, but I believe that God does and will forgive you and give you a second chance. If you have already had sex, first confess it. Then surrender the struggle to God. Pray for and have self-control. Recommit your purity to Christ and stay pure from here on out. Don't stay trapped in the same sin. You can be a born again virgin. He will forgive you...you'll always be God's baby.

- *Don't dress to kill.* You deserve a guy who wants you for more than your looks. And you don't want to cause your brother to stumble either.

- *Don't ever change for a boy.* I want someone who sees beyond my flaws and imperfections because, let's be honest, they exist. If I do something nerdy or stupid in front of my boyfriend, he just laughs at me and smiles. I look up in his eyes and say, "Uh...I'm such a nerd!" He looks down in my eyes and says, "Yeah...but you're my nerd." I love moments like that. A person who really loves you looks beyond the imperfections and sees the beauty within because you are a mystery worth solving. Don't ever compromise. Don't be ordinary. Don't ever change for a boy.

- *Don't ever replace your friends with a guy.* I love hanging out with my best friend. We are so crazy and laugh continually at each other. I remember when we went out TP-ing one night; we were petrified! A cat jumped on her car and set the car alarm off. It was a hilarious disaster! I love her. I can always count on her, be myself, and I know she will always love me! You need a friend in your life like that. One who will encourage you and keep you accountable. If you are struggling with being too sexy, having sex, or staying in a bad relationship, I'm challenging you to confide in a girlfriend you can trust. It's important to remember that guys will never replace your friends.

Of those teens who have not yet had sex:

- 6% said they would have sex before finishing high school
- 8% said they are waiting to have sex until they are out of high school
- 42% said they are waiting to have sex until they are in a committed relationship
- 37% said they are waiting until marriage
- 8% didn't know when they would have sex[5]

Of the teens, ages 15-17, who were asked about the benefits of waiting to have sex:

- 93% reported waiting out of respect for themselves
- 91% reported waiting to stay in control of the relationship
- 91% reported waiting to get respect from parents
- 91% reported waiting to keep true to their religious values
- 84% reported waiting to get respect from friends
- 79% reported waiting so they did not have to worry about pregnancy or STDs
- 78% reported it was just one less thing to worry about[6]

Listening to Dad

- *Save yourself.* You'll never regret holding out until marriage to have sex. Some may say you're boring and old-fashioned, but I have never met a Christian woman who wished she hadn't waited. And I've met many who made mistakes early in life who wish they *had* waited for marriage to have sex.

- *Be beautiful.* Take care of your body. Enjoy and nurture what God has given you. You'll soon learn that great sex never starts in the bedroom. It's about who you are as a person and embracing sex as a wonderful expression of your love in marriage.

- *An audience of One.* One truth that has always helped me is this: I'm never alone. God is always there, and He sees everything. He can help and encourage you too! You will need His strength to stand strong.

- *If you mess up—and I pray you don't—know that God and I*

love you. His message is clear in 1 John 1:9. God promises to forgive and wash you clean. Consequences? Sure. But freedom is in confessing it to Him, asking for forgiveness, and connecting to a new life of freedom in Him. God is always there for you. So am I.

Crazy Emotions

Feelings come from your heart and can tell you the state
of your relationships...But the point is, your feelings
are your responsibility and you must own them and
see them as your problem so you can begin to find an
answer to whatever issue they are pointing to.
–Dr. Henry Cloud and Dr. John Townsend, *Boundaries*

Ever been asked to go out with a guy that one of your friends knew? You know...the boy everybody thinks would be your perfect match? You get excited, and just when you think you can actually trust your friends' judgment, you finally meet the guy and you two have nothing in common. It's a disaster. What were they thinking?

When I was in tenth grade, one of my best friends and her boyfriend wanted to meet up with a guy they knew—a guy I'd seen before and thought was cute. So they set us up for a double date at the movies.

On the day of the date, I was really nervous. The boys were going to meet us at the theater. On the way there, my friend tried to calm my nerves, but I was still a mess. As I walked toward the building, my heart thumped. The closer I got, the faster my heart beat. When I made the grand entrance into the theater, I couldn't believe it. He was standing there waiting, and he looked so cute! I thought, *Maybe my friends really do know what they're talking about.*

That's when I found out how much my friends really did love me.

"Hi, Megan," he said, "I didn't know you were coming."

"What! Hello! You didn't say anything?" My mind raced...my heart fluttered...I couldn't believe it. I didn't know what to say. I was embarrassed. And my friends...well, I am not sure what they were thinking. My friends told him that I liked him but didn't tell him I was going to be at the movie. Awkward. He avoided me the entire night! He didn't even sit next to me. As soon as the movie was over, he literally ran out of the theater to avoid talking to me. So much for getting to know him. He wanted nothing to do with me.

I liked him and thought he was cute. And he ran away from me! I felt like I had a big red light on me flashing in front of everybody: Rejected! Rejected! Rejected! I was so embarrassed. What was wrong with me? Was it my hair? A protruding blemish on my face? Something I said? Something I was wearing? I couldn't figure out what I had done.

When I told my mom what happened, she asked what was wrong with him. I replied, "No, Mom, you don't get it. It's not about him... it's about what's wrong with me."

Mom corrected me, "Megan, he's the child for running away. At least you stuck around."

I then realized how often we immediately react to our emotions in self-defeating ways. I *felt* rejected. And that feeling of rejection automatically translated in my mind as, "Something is wrong with *me*." And when something is wrong with *me*, I have to figure out how to fix it.

Here's a classic example. I was recently reading an issue of a popular magazine for girls. One of the survey questions asked, "How many of you have silently vowed to give up cookies after you saw a celeb looking good in her skinny jeans?"

Whoa! That's me! I've done that! Yes, I admit it. I gave up sweets... to look like a skinny, size zero celeb. Not one of my finest moments, but I think we all struggle with it to some degree.

Until I talked to my mom about the situation with Mr. Scaredy Cat, I didn't even think about how embarrassed *he* was, or the fact that he didn't know what to do with such a beautiful girl (smile). It just took me a while to understand what he was missing.

What Are Emotions?

The best way of forgetting how you think you feel is
to concentrate on what you know you know.
−Mary Stewart

So what are emotions? These are the things that make my body change in weird ways—my heart beats faster, I sweat, or I blush in front of everybody at exactly the time I *don't* want to blush! I hate it when I lose control of anything—let alone bodily functions!

But I think that's why we tend to fear our emotions—*we are afraid of losing control.* The feeling of rejection at the movie automatically translated into this thought, *What's wrong with me?* When there's something wrong with me, I have to fix it to regain control. It's like my body was screaming at me, *There's something wrong!* On the other hand, if the boy would have stayed at the movie theater and sat next to me, I may have felt accepted by him. Feeling accepted calms me. Makes me think I'm in control and that there's nothing wrong.

Where does this roller coaster of emotional chaos come from? How can I feel one way this minute and another way the next? What's to blame? You guessed it—hormones!

Think of the feeling you get when your brother or sister runs to Mom or Dad to "one up" you and get you in trouble? What are you feeling? Agitated? Eager to get revenge? I do! That's because *adrenaline* rushes through your body and puts it on high alert, warning you that things are out of control.

But when you're the one who calls out your brother or sister and they're in trouble, what do you feel? Happy. Elated. Joyful! That's because *endorphins* wash over your brain with a calming effect that tells you everything is just fine.

List of Emotions		
Love	Happiness	Anger
Sadness	Fear	Disgust
Surprise	Joy	Shame
Dislike	Interest	Guilt
Distress	Worry	Depressed
Anxious	Acceptance	Grateful
Lonely	Jealous	Pity
Melancholy	Content	Confident

So basically when we're depressed and want to eat ice cream, cookies, chocolate, and potato chips—I mean the whole bag of chips—we can blame it on our hormones. As teenagers, hormones are more likely to cause our emotions to change than when we were children or when we become adults. Not only that, the brainiacs who do research have finally discovered that teenagers are more likely to experience the joy of the moment than to think through how their actions now will affect the future.[1]

No kidding! I don't need a doctor or scientist to tell me that. It's like Cameron Diaz said: "Believe me, you can get into a lot of trouble being sixteen years old in a foreign country with no adult telling you when to come home." Better her than me.

When we're growing up, it's tough to think about the consequences of our behavior, especially if we have to choose between what feels right and what feels wrong. It's hard to understand that emotions are temporary. They come and go. Not only that, they are not always accurate. What you perceive to be true and what really is true can be completely different. You can be sincere, but sincerely wrong.

For instance, if I believed that boy rejected me because I was fat or unattractive, I can sincerely give up cookies and sweets because I think doing so will make me *feel* prettier and more accepted. But the problem is I can't always trust my feelings. What happened in the theater had more to do with him than me. I can give up sweets to feel better about myself, but I would be sincerely wrong. There's more to my identity than my outward appearance.

Reacting Versus Responding

It's Saturday night and everybody is hanging out at the bowling alley until 9 p.m., and then going to the movies for the 9:30 show. You're not really sure who will be there, other than a few of your friends from school. Your parents tell you that you're allowed only to go to the bowling alley and the movie theater, and then you are to come directly home. If you go anywhere else, you must call them.

What are you thinking? *Why can't my parents ever trust me?* You're immediately defensive and *feel* angry because they don't trust you. You initially agree to their rules, but as you leave for the evening, you get really quiet because you *feel* as if your parents are never going to allow you to grow up and make your own decisions.

When you arrive at the bowling alley, there are people in your group you don't know. One guy in particular is the life of the crowd and a friend of one of your close friends. You really enjoy his humor and the company of the others as well. But when it comes time to go to the theater, the "new guy" decides to invite everybody over to his house to watch a movie instead—because his parents aren't home. The feeling you had toward your parents at the beginning of the evening becomes an attitude you carry with you all night long. You're still upset that your parents don't trust you. You're unsure about whether or not they will let you go to the boy's house because they don't know him. So you decide not to call and to go ahead anyway.

Let's look back on this for a moment. You plan to be with some friends. You are on good terms with your parents. All is well. Then they tell you they want you to do *only* what you told them, and if you go against that plan, you *must* call them. Something rises up in you...ugh...they don't trust you! You *feel* angry and upset at them. *Afraid* they will say no to going with the group to the "new guy's" house. You decide to disobey them. Your emotion trumped your decision.

What if all goes well? You go to his house, watch a movie, and then go home. Nothing bad happens. Mom and Dad never find out. All is well. Likely scenario.

But let's say it doesn't go down that way. What if somebody in your group tells their parents they went to this boy's house, and their parents tell your parents, and now you're caught? Consequences = Grounded. Oh yeah, and your parents end up trusting you a lot less than they did before! Also a likely scenario.

But what if something really bad happens at this guy's house. You get into a situation where everybody is doing something you're not comfortable with. Maybe they pull out the alcohol...or worse yet, drugs. Now you're somewhere you're not supposed to be with people you and your parents don't even know, and peer pressure is sinking in. You now *feel* inferior and wimpy because you're not giving in and participating in the activities of others. For crying out loud, you just wanted to watch a movie.

You have to live with the decisions you make. If you make decisions based on your emotions, you'll often find yourself left with a decision you can't live with—but have to.

When Can I Trust Emotions?

We often live by our emotions. They shape our personality, affect the decisions we make, and influence our interactions with others. They can be gut reactions that fuel our behavior, but living with crazy emotions can be very difficult. On one hand I see girls who allow their emotions to run their lives, and on the other I see girls who completely deny their emotions.

The girl who allows her emotions to run her life is a drama waiting to happen. Everything is a crisis.

Watch this. Let's call her Dana-the-Drama-Queen. Dana-the-Drama-Queen sees Bobby walking into school with Andrea one morning. She thinks that means that Bobby likes Andrea so she starts talking about it. As soon as it "gets out" that Bobby walked with Andrea into school, Jason finds out. Jason is Andrea's boyfriend. Now Jason wants to fight Bobby after school for trying to steal his girlfriend. But because Dana-the-Drama-Queen likes Bobby, she now hates Andrea for hitting on him. Before you know it, Dana-the-Drama-Queen hates Andrea, Andrea hates her, and Bobby and Jason are fighting at the flagpole after school. And all because it just so happened that Bobby and Andrea arrived at school at the same time this morning. Nothing more. Nothing less. Imagine the gossip going on at school because of this mess!

If you're like me, when the alarm clock goes off in the morning, you hit the snooze button...again and again and again. That alarm clock is telling us it's time to do something—get out of bed. When we don't listen to the alarm clock, there is a consequence. Either we are late for school or work. Or worse yet, our mom or dad gets fed up with the annoying buzzer and comes to drag us out of bed.

My emotions are like an internal alarm clock that goes off to tell me it's time to do something with my relationships. With my relationship with my boyfriend. My parents. My friends. Or my teachers. They warn me that something may not be right with those I am in relationship with. If I don't listen to them or hit the "snooze" button on them, things can get ugly real quick.

What do I mean by ugly? Take the guy you are dating. What happens when he chooses his buddies over you on Friday night? How do you feel? What emotions are triggered inside of you? Anger? Sadness? Jealousy? And if you aren't dating anyone, there's probably some guy who repeatedly turns his attention from you and focuses it on another girl. What do you feel? Anger? Rejection? Embarrassment? Jealousy? See, we get to these emotions one way or another!

In an experiment, teenage girls were beeped at random times of the day and asked what was going on and had they had any strong experiences of feeling recently.

- 34% reported that they were thinking about real or fantasized relationships with boys
- 25% said they were thinking about romantic relationships[2]

Boyfriend or no boyfriend, how you handle those feelings, as we saw earlier with Dana-the-Drama-Queen, can make or break your relationship.

Some girls will actually just submit to boys out of fear of losing them. They lose their own sense of who they are and stop giving their opinions because they are afraid of being dropped by their boyfriends. When you ignore your feelings and allow him to walk all over you...it can lead to depression. For more than a year, teenage girls were monitored for depression and romantic involvement. Once a girl got into a romantic relationship, she got more depressed. This was especially true of the younger girls.[3]

The Cry of Our Hearts

Tears are the safety valve of the heart when
too much pressure is laid on it.
—ALBERT SMITH

Ever have days when all you want to do is cry? To just go home, lie in bed, and bawl your eyes out? Even for no reason at all? I have. Sometimes a good cry feels good—no matter what the reason for the tears. Whether it's that time of the month, you're having trouble in your relationships, or you're not in your devotions, there are all kinds of reasons why we cry.

One thing I've come to learn about myself is that I usually cry because I feel lonely. When this happens, I sometimes feel guilty. *Why should I feel lonely?* I ask myself. I have wonderful friends and an amazing family, all who dearly love me. Yet I still feel lonely. At times I think we all do.

However, in the midst of the loneliness, I don't want my boyfriend or my parents to become more important than God. I don't want to be dependent on them for my happiness. To rely on them for my self-worth. To turn only to them when I am hurting. To allow the people God has placed in my life to dictate how I feel about myself. This is probably the biggest struggle I face.

But why the guilt for feeling lonely? I mean...come on...God designed us for relationship! He placed the longing to be loved in our hearts. And He places our closest friends and family in our lives so we can feel connected—first to Him and then to one another. Jesus said, "Love the Lord your God with all your heart and with all your soul and with all your mind." Then secondly He said to "Love your neighbor as yourself" (Matthew 22:37,39).

I believe the more connected we are to one another, the more connected we become to the Father—because we come to feel His love and pain for us in the context of relationships. For it's in relationships that we love. In relationships we hurt. And in relationships we feel. Our emotions are directly tied to our relationships.

Crazy Little Thing Called Love

*There are three kinds of love: instinctual, emotional, and
conscious love. There is no challenge in the first two;
they precede from human biology and frailty.*

–Warren Cooley

God said, "It's not good for the man to be alone" (Genesis 2:18).
We were designed for relationships. It's natural to want to be liked
and loved, but too often when we want to be liked and loved, we go
to extremes to get it. And when we manipulate other people to be
liked, we wrong ourselves and those we manipulate. We hunger to
be noticed. Touched. Held. Cared for. You want somebody to love
you. And it's a good thing. But it's bad when we manipulate others
to get it.

When it comes to loving and being loved, you've got to settle it
in your heart or you will compromise everything about you. You
will settle for things you don't want or that are not good for you.
The more you crave attention, the more you seek it, going to more
places looking for it...even places you shouldn't.

When author Josh McDowell came to our school to speak about
relationships, he said that 37 percent of evangelical born-again students believe that if you truly love someone, it makes premarital
sex okay. That means more than one in every three evangelical,
born-again Christians reading this book believe it is okay to have
sex outside of marriage as long as you truly love the person you're
with. It's a shame we are ignoring God's truth just so that we can
feel good.

My mom and I have the "love" conversation over and over again.
She tells me that I am too young to understand true love. I must
say that as hesitant as I was to agree with her, I now think I am
beginning to understand what she means.

Josh McDowell confirmed it. He said that 98 percent of

Christians cannot define love. So how do we know what it means to "truly love" somebody?

- 72% of teens think they are mature enough to really fall in love.
- 15% do not think they are mature enough to fall in love.
- 12% are not sure.[4]

Your Big Brother's Thoughts on...
Being Giddy and Twitterpated

Megan,

You hang on every word he says. Daydream about your wedding day. Pick the petals off the flower as you recite the words, "He loves me. He loves me not." You've caught yourself doing this. I know that because it's the heart cry of most every girl I've ever met—to fall in love.

But be careful. The early stages of a relationship are—amazing! Hanging with him every moment you can. Texting and calling him when you're not able to see him. And then there are the feelings you get when you're with him—you know what I'm talking about—the giddy and twitterpated feelings of knowing you're cherished. Those can be dangerous!

"How dangerous?" you might ask. Consider this: Being in love triggers the same part of the brain as cocaine. Yes...the feelings of love in the early stages of a relationship are like being on cocaine. And it's addicting. When your boyfriend drops those three most coveted words, "I love you," what happens to you inside? What do you do? Move a little closer to him. Hold him a little tighter. And melt. But be careful not to define love based on these early feelings

of relational bliss. Love cannot be defined by the feelings you get in the first six months of a relationship. They'll eventually wear off. I have heard too many stories of heartbroken girls who literally run to their girlfriends crying, "But he said he loved me!"

Remember, Megan, choosing who you marry is the biggest decision you'll make next to salvation, and love is not based on feelings alone. Guard your heart. And be careful not to allow those amazing feelings you get early in the relationship to cloud any wise decisions you should make about the boy you are dating. These decisions will stay with you for a lifetime.

With brotherly love,
Josh

What's a Girl To Do?

Control your emotion or it will control you.
—UNKNOWN

Because "the heart is hopelessly dark and deceitful, a puzzle that no one can figure out" (Jeremiah 17:9 MSG), I pray that you do not trust your emotions anytime soon. We must think before we act, no matter what our feelings are telling us.

Paul says, "Do not be anxious about anything" (Philippians 4:6) and "In your anger, do not sin" (Ephesians 4:26). He doesn't say do not get angry. He says, "Do not sin in your anger."

- *Remain in the Word every day.* As I process this whole idea of emotional control in my life, I learn that I need God's daily guidance. We all need to "commit [our] actions to the LORD" (Proverbs 16:3 NLT) because "[His] thoughts are not your thoughts, nor are your ways [His] ways" (Isaiah 55:8). When somebody wrongs me, or I feel rejected or hurt in any way, I need to take a step back and pray before I act. The only way I can truly make the right decision, in spite of what I am feeling, is to know what the Bible says about what I should do. "For the word of God is alive and powerful. It is sharper than the sharpest two-edged sword, cutting between soul and spirit, between joint and marrow. It exposes our innermost thoughts and desires. Nothing in all creation is hidden from God. Everything is naked and exposed before his eyes, and he is the one to whom we are accountable" (Hebrews 4:12-13 NLT).

- *Don't trust your emotions because most of the time they are temporary.* You have to live with the decisions you make. If you make them because of a high or low emotion, you'll find that after the emotion wears off, you're left with a decision you probably don't want to live with, but have to.

- *Don't let your fears control your decisions.* I think we all live with fear. Fear of abandonment. The uncertainty of the future. Failure. Even the fear of not being in control. But when you let your fears guide your decisions, you will make wrong ones. For example, if your fear of how your boyfriend will react is stopping you from breaking up with him, you're making a fear-based decision that could affect your entire life. Do you want to settle for less just because you fear somebody else's reaction?

- *Don't get stuck.* When you're in a relationship for a while, it's hard to get out of it because you get used to being with somebody. The security of having someone rules the day and can rule your mind and heart. Don't replace God's security and comfort with that of anyone else.

My friends tell me about the tears they shed in the silence of their bedrooms or in the spray of the shower. They want to be loved just like I do. I can't help but think how much God really wants to be loved. How much He wants to be loved by us.

Listening to Dad

- *Know how much God loves you.* He is the only one who can fill your heart. No guy will ever do that.

- *Love will come.* Don't force it to happen, rush it, or be consumed by it. I know it can be frustrating and discouraging, but God will work out the details in His proper time.

- *Pray for your future husband every day.* Pray that God will work in his life to protect him and build him up to be the godly husband you deserve. I am.

- *Meditate on 1 Corinthians 13 often.* This is known as the great love chapter in the Bible. It describes what love is and isn't.

- *When you are loved you'll feel safe.* If you feel threatened or unsafe in any way in your relationship, then something's wrong. That's when you need to reach out for help.

> *Overeagerness to marry is most often associated with the deep and powerful excitement that bubbles up around impending marriage...A lifetime decision like marriage requires a clear, unhurried mind.*
> –Dr. Neil Clark Warren [5]

When Life's Not Fair

I am responsible. Although I may not be able to prevent the worst
from happening, I am responsible for my attitude toward the
inevitable misfortunes that darken life. Bad things do happen;
how I respond to them defines my character and the quality of
my life. I can choose to sit in perpetual sadness, immobilized
by the gravity of my loss, or I can choose to rise from the
pain and treasure the most precious gift I have—life itself.
—WALTER ANDERSON

One day Pete, a normal college kid with light brown hair and brown eyes with an "American Eagle" look, was forced to finally tell his parents the bad news. Sitting down to the computer with shaky hands and an uncomfortable feeling, he began typing the email he didn't want to write.

> Mom and Dad,
>
> Please know that I love you both very much. Before you read this email, I want you to sit down...unless you already are. I am sorry I didn't call this week. It's just been crazy. Last week my roommates had a party here at school, and things got a little out of control. It wasn't that bad at all, I promise. But the police came. My roommates were cited for underage drinking. I swear I am not lying when I say this, but I only had one beer—and they arrested me. I couldn't believe it. I don't get drunk, Mom. The next day when I went to leave the apartment, I backed into another

lady's car. It wasn't that bad though. Since I am on your insurance, they are paying for it. The rest of the week has been fine. Oh, except that Amber, the girl I told you about, who I met a few weeks ago? We found out yesterday she is pregnant. You are going to be grandparents! I will call you in a few days.

Love,

Pete

P.S. Nothing in this email is true, except that I failed my finance class and have to retake it.

Pete had to tell his parents he failed a class. He figured by comparing the F to what his life could be like, his parents might be a little easier on him about the failing grade.

Putting Life into Perspective

Death is not the greatest loss in life. The greatest loss is what dies inside us while we live.

–NORMAN COUSINS

Zits. Bad hair days. Crabby friends. Fat days. Schoolwork. And of course, annoying little brothers. If only everyday problems like these were all we had to worry about. For some of the fortunate few reading this book, this is the extent of the pain in your life so far. But I promise you...it will get worse. For others reading this book, you know the pain life sometimes has to offer.

Maybe you're picked on in school. Maybe your family struggles financially. Maybe you wear secondhand clothes and other kids tease you because of it. What about the locker room during gym class? Are you fearful of what others think? Didn't make the team? Are you always picked last...or so it seems?

Some of you have been hurt worse. Divorce. Abandonment.

Betrayal from those who are supposed to love you. Verbal and emotional abuse. Even sexual abuse. As I get older, I can't believe the hurt some of my dearest friends have experienced. Pain—I am learning—comes wrapped in a lot of different packages.

The Day God Rattled My Perspective

*I've never tried to block out the memories of the
past, even though some are painful. I don't understand
people who hide from their past. Everything you live
through helps to make you the person you are now.*

–Sophia Loren

I'll never forget the day—November fifth—the evening our high school choir provided the special music for the Sunday night service at our home church. We enjoyed singing together—our performances had received rave reviews from around the country. We were excited to perform for the people who truly knew and loved us. We just knew it was going to be great.

The brisk fall air outside could not chill the warmth that was felt inside the church with all of our families present. Each song seemed to flow throughout the audience with a warm message of love and hope. Touched by the glorious harmony of students' voices lifted in praise to God, I gently reached over and grasped the hand of one of my lifelong friends, Jen Barrick, who was standing beside me. She looked over at me with her beautiful smile, made eye contact, and continued to belt out notes with more enthusiasm and passion than ever.

What I didn't know in that moment was how life can change in an instant. It would be the last time I remembered Jen as the beautiful, intelligent, and aspiring young woman of promise *I thought* she was destined to be. She had everything going for her. Kind. Gregarious. Outgoing. Captain of the cheerleading squad. An excellent student. A loving family.

On her way home from church that night, everything changed. A drunk driver careened into her family's van at a speed in excess of 70 miles per hour. Jen suffered a traumatic head injury and almost died. Sitting at the University of Virginia Medical Center that night, I thought it would be the last time I saw Jen alive.

Journal Entry
(10 days after the accident)

Sorry I haven't written in a while. Right now I feel like I need God's touch and blessing in my life. I want to be on fire so bad, but right now it just seems like life is hard, and in reality it is. Today was actually good. I mean I was really happy today. I got to see Linda (Jen's mom) for the first time, and it was so sweet to see Josh (Jen's brother) embrace her and kiss her all over her face. This whole accident has made me realize how short life is and how thankful I am for God's blessings in my life.

Just reading the Bible calms my spirit. I feel God beside me! Thank you, Lord, for being here in the midst of my trials and loneliness. I love you!

Jen is still unconscious. Now it's not a matter of life or death, but a fear of the unknown. In many ways this whole situation is hard to understand, but God is using Jen in a powerful way! I hope I am always a helping hand and a joy to God and others because I want Him to use me. Every breath of life He gives me I know I don't deserve. Lord, your love is extravagant! Keep me safe and close in your arms, Jesus...

Life Ain't Always Beautiful

> *God, who foresaw your tribulation, has specially armed*
> *you to go through it, not without pain but without stain.*
>
> –C.S. Lewis

Josh, Jen's younger brother, was the least injured of all four family members and was released from the hospital earlier than his parents and sister. Everything was difficult because Josh's mom, Linda; his dad, Andy; and his sister, Jen, were all in different hospitals because of the nature of their injuries. Traveling to each hospital to tend to and care for each was grueling for all involved. As a result, Josh came to live with us for a while.

I'll never forget a time shortly after the accident when my dad was driving down the road with Josh, Zach, my younger brother, and me in the car. Our family loves country music and when Gary Allan's song came across the radio, we all quieted down and listened to the words of "Life Ain't Always Beautiful" (but it's a beautiful ride). As I looked over at Josh, I could tell he was listening intently to the song.

Then he said, "That's kind of like us right now, isn't it, Coach Tim?"

My dad looked back at him through the rearview mirror and with a soft voice said, "Yeah. You're right, Josh. But God did a miracle. You all should have died—He will help you through."

And He is. Jen is home now. While she has new challenges and uphill battles ahead, she is recovering. Different? Yes. Just as beautiful? No. In her own way, she is *more* beautiful today than ever before. God sees her beauty, and those around us have been privileged to see it too.

Our Hurting Generation

A few months ago my senior class went on a hayride and then sat around a bonfire together at a local camp near our high school. The snap, crackle, and pop of the flickering fire at the center of the circle drew our attention, but not the focus of conversation. My friends shared stories that night—stories that most others in the group were unaware of. Stories of heartache. Pain. Hurt. The openness of one led to the vulnerability of another...and before you knew it, one by one, my friends began talking about who they were, what they were going through, and how they felt about the class, family, and friends. Many said they were distant from God. Most didn't know how to reconnect with Him. Others had been deeply hurt by family members who were supposed to love them.

Sad Eyes

- 33% of teenage women report sexual abuse.

- Abuse often starts in childhood (fondling, explicit nudity, suggestive comments) but becomes more direct and invasive with adolescence (rape).[1]

- Girls are more likely than boys to have their perpetrator be a relative or family friend.

- The average age of the onset of abuse is seven to eight years old, and it usually goes on for two years.

- As adolescents and adults, victims are more likely to get sick more frequently, have more guy friends, be suicidal, self-injure, have sex earlier, have more sexual partners in adolescence, be revictimized (raped), and be depressed or anxious.[2]

During that night of sharing, nobody felt how freezing cold it really was outside. We were all lost in the depths of one another's heartache. And although not everybody got a chance to share that night, those who did were glad for the opportunity.

At the end of the evening when my dad picked me up, I thanked him for being there for me throughout my life. I realized that night how good I really had it. My class—my closest friends—were hurting more than I had ever imagined.

I think Jen's life is an example of this—a clear picture of where our generation is today. Filled with potential, opportunity, and promise, from innovations in technology, medicine, athletics, and the arts to name a few, we have more possibilities than ever before to impact our culture and make a difference in the world around us. But where there's potential, danger always seems to lurk close behind.

Youth is also seen as a time of transition, recklessness, and poor decision making. But for many teens, like a lot of my friends, it is a sad time. A season that robs them of the very life they dream of. And they walk around trying to fake a smile.

Impact of Divorce on Girls

- Girls are affected the most by divorce in the areas of educational attainment and in their adult romantic relationships.
- Girls in step families were more likely to struggle with anxiety and depression than girls from intact families.
- Girls from divorced families have poorer quality of relationships with their dads, perceive their fathers care about them less, and see their fathers less than girls from intact families.
- Girls tend to blame themselves for their parents' divorce.[3]

Did you know that teen suicide has become the third leading cause of death among our age group?[4] The United States also ranks among the highest in the world for students who do not feel generally happy with their lives—many of our peers feel lonely. But I believe it's more than that. Much of this brokenness seems to be related to the challenges and often tragic breakdown of relationships, particularly when there's no dad. For instance, nearly 40 percent of America's kids will wake up in a home tomorrow where their biological father does not live.[5] Fatherless homes account for

63 percent of youth suicides, 90 percent of homeless and runaway children, 71 precent of high school dropouts, 85 percent of youths in prison, and well over 50 percent of teen mothers.[6]

If any of these things are part of your immediate world, I want you to know you are not alone—and you can make it through.

But It's a Beautiful Ride...

> *Take your everyday, ordinary life—your sleeping,*
> *eating, going-to-work, and walking-around life—and*
> *place it before God as an offering. Embracing what God*
> *does for you is the best thing you can do for him.*
> Romans 12:1 msg

I believe that even during deep sadness, all is not lost. Most of the kids I know want something more. I believe we long to be honest about the issues of our lives, to have friends, to connect with people—to be relational in a world of promise and great opportunity. Multibillion dollar websites like Facebook.com and MySpace.com scream for relational connectedness and community.

Come to think of it, one of the greatest lessons of my life did not come in an academic setting. It came while in the great classroom of life, observing what others did for Jen. As I watched friends, family, and professionals work tirelessly together to care for a human soul and restore dignity in the midst of tragedy, I learned that life, although broken, scarred, and fragile, is more precious and meaningful than personal accolades and accomplishments. The great story here is not about Jen's potential, it was about her person. I learned more about life and how and why we matter by simply being present.

Jen Barrick's life, the life she now lives, teaches me about the common good of what and who we are as human beings. As Ernest Hemingway once said, "Every man's life ends the same way. It is only the details of how he lived and how he died that distinguish one man from another."

Now I think I understand the difference between teaching a subject like math and teaching students. We need relationships—invested parents, role models, friends, and mentors—in our lives. If you don't have a good role model, somebody who is mentoring you through life's difficult times, I suggest you find somebody you can trust and ask them to walk through life and the Word of God with you.

We all need it. It's what life is all about. One girl helping another—all for a common good.

Your Big Brother's Thoughts on...
Character

Megan,

A few years ago I realized that the one thing we have to hang onto forever—the one thing people will remember about us—is our character. Not our possessions. Not even our accomplishments. They'll remember the way you treated others and the way you handled life's difficulties.

This realization led me on a soul-searching venture to discover true character. But what I found disturbed me—true character is molded in hard times. I didn't like that! I read verses like Romans 5:3-4, "We know that suffering produces perseverance; perseverance, character; and character, hope." And James 1:2-4, "The testing of your faith produces perseverance [and] perseverance must finish its work so that you may be mature."

When trials come that test our faith—and they will—what will you do with them? Learn from them? Fight through them? Or will you whine? Quit? Blame others? Succumb to the pressure?

Maybe you think the situation you're going through is hopeless. Change your thoughts. "Against all hope, Abraham in hope believed and so became the father of many nations"(Romans 4:18). Even when Abraham's situation seemed hopeless, he believed in it...and persevered!

I like what Andy Andrews wrote about adversity. He said, "Don't ask, 'Why me?' Instead ask, 'Why not me?'"[7] You want to do something great in life? Turn life's challenges into opportunities for greatness. Take the situations that seem hopeless and own them. Believe in the hope, persevere through the trials, and the whole character thing will take care of itself.

Why not you?
Josh

The Road Less Traveled

*If we deny love that is given to us, if we refuse
to give love because we fear pain or loss, then
our lives will be empty, our loss greater.*
–AUTHOR UNKNOWN

The Bible, when referring to salvation, says that the path to destruction is paved with a broad road and a wide gate. Many people enter through it and live lives of destruction and bad choices. But the road to life is narrow, with a small gate that very few enter (Matthew 7:13-14).

Bitter or Better

The Barricks had to choose. And they chose the narrow road. Not that it was easy...it never is. In fact choosing the narrow road is more difficult. That's why fewer people go there. "Don't look for shortcuts to God. The market is flooded with surefire, easygoing formulas for a successful life that can be practiced in your spare time. Don't fall for that stuff, even though crowds of people do. The way to life—to God!—is vigorous and requires total attention" (Matthew 7:13-14 MSG).

Choosing to live with the love of God in your heart, even when you hurt, will make a difference in your life and in the lives of those around you. I have seen countless people come to know Christ's love through the Barrick family since the accident.

What do you do when you are hurt or have been violated? When life's not the way it's supposed to be? When your family is messed up? Or your closest friend moves away? Or someone you love dies?

What do you do when life just isn't fair?

No matter what has happened to you in life, the road you choose is yours. You can choose to live the better way, with the love of Jesus in your heart, or you can choose the bitter way, a life not reflective of the power of Christ. Either way you choose, the Bible says "You will recognize them by their fruits" (Matthew 7:20 ESV). You have to choose a path—continue toward pain or discover the road to healing.

I'll never forget when Papa (my mom's dad) died. I was his first grandchild—which meant I was closer to him than the others. His death really hurt me. He would call me his "little angel." I remember the night before he died. I was ten. I had just gotten vaccination shots in my arm and my grandmother thought it would be better if I didn't see him because of the live virus in me. I sat in the car and cried. It's like I knew he was going to die...like this would be my last chance to see him. And it was. He died the next day.

I was the only grandchild allowed at the viewing, and Papa's death deeply affected me. All of a sudden death became real. I started to think about life a little differently. Though I was saved at four or five years old, I don't remember it very well. At age 11, challenged by the permanency of death, I knew I wanted to make the commitment to serve God for the rest of my life. And that's what I did. Four months after Papa's death, I rededicated my life to Christ.

I had to choose whether or not I was going to be mad at the world and God for my grandfather's death. And sometimes I believe that it's okay to be angry...as long as you work through that anger to a path of healing and reconciliation with whomever it is you are angry at. But ultimately we can choose to stay in our pain, in our anger and our hurt, or we can choose to work through that to a place of healing and freedom.

Think about this for a moment. My dad says often, "Your past is not your past if it's affecting your present." Are you still angry about something that's happened in your life?

If you're really hurting and don't know where to turn, I beg you to talk to your mom or dad, your pastor, a mentor, or a girlfriend you can trust. If people have hurt or abused you in deeper ways sexually or emotionally, you may need to find a Christian counselor to help you for a while. There are good people out there who love and want to help us! Not everybody thinks we are all crazy. As broken people living in a broken world, we all need counseling to some degree or another. As my dad always says, "You can't heal what you don't feel." You've got to talk openly about it. The more hurt we've experienced usually means the more help we need.

Does God Really Care?

> If with heart and soul you're doing good, do you think you can be
> stopped? Even if you suffer for it, you're still better off. Don't give
> the opposition a second thought. Through thick and thin, keep
> your hearts at attention, in adoration before Christ, your Master.
> 1 PETER 3:13-15 MSG

When life isn't fair, it's easy to believe that God doesn't care. But the underlying issue is whether we trust Him or not. I think that so many times our fear of God is not as it should be. He is someone we are literally afraid of. Being afraid of Him, though, makes it tough to relate to Him. Think about it. How well do you relate with people you're afraid of? They're not approachable! We stay away from them. And the more we stay away from them, the less we know their true character.

I like to think I fear God in a good way, that is with awe and wonder like Moses when he said to the Israelites, "Don't be afraid. God has come to test you and instill a deep and reverent awe within you so that you won't sin" (Exodus 20:20 MSG). Living with a healthy fear of God is about being wowed by Him! Living in such awe so that it hurts me to sin against Him. But knowing that when I do, He is compassionate (2 Corinthians 1:3-4), forgiving (Colossians 2:13-14), and I can trust that He will have my best interest in *all* circumstances (Matthew 6:25-34). Kind of like my earthly dad. I fear him. I don't want to let him down. But when I do, he is a comfort, and I know I can trust that he cares about me.

I hate it when people blame God for their problems. Even Jesus had problems. Big time problems! He was beaten, whipped, spit on, ridiculed, and hung on a cross—literally crying out in pain over you and me.

He has given us more mercy than we ever deserve. "It's a wonder God didn't lose his temper and do away with the whole lot of us. Instead, immense in mercy and with an incredible love, he embraced us" (Ephesians 2:3-5 MSG). He gave us life. He is the Creator of all that is good. I wish more people understood that.

God loves you so much that He chose to give you life (John 3:16). Just because there is bad in the world doesn't mean God doesn't love you. The Bible says that He is the healer of the heartbroken. He bandages your wounds (Psalm 147:3). He really is there for you and will mend your brokenness...even a broken heart.

What's a Girl To Do?

> *God is there, ready to help; I'm fearless no*
> *matter what. Who or what can get to me?*
> –HEBREWS 13:6 MSG

Learning to trust God can be very difficult, especially if you have been hurt by other people who were supposed to love you. I thank God for my parents because they have taught me that God is safe and that I really can trust Him (2 Samuel 7:28; Psalm 62:8).

- *Surrender.* Whatever has happened to you, whatever trials and temptations you have faced, surrender them all to God. You cannot move forward if you're hanging onto the pain.

- *Learn to trust God.* For those of you who are afraid or don't know how to trust God, start by simply telling Him of your fears, concerns, and desire to trust Him. If you need direction on how to trust Him, begin by asking Him. You won't understand what God wants to do in your life and sufferings if you aren't talking to Him. You have to pray.

- *Read the Bible.* Again, you won't understand what God is doing in your life if you don't know His character. Get a daily devotional and read it along with the Bible every day. I tell you...I struggle just like everyone else with doing my devotions. But I am happiest when I am in them. As John Piper said, "God is most glorified, when we are most satisfied in Him."

Listening to Dad

- *Rain falls on the just and unjust.* You will experience hard times. Problems are not the issue—it's what you do with them that will determine your future.

- *Talk it through with people you love and are close to.* We were not designed to walk through life alone. Turn to those you trust and let them help you.

- *Know the Truth.* To make it through hard times, you have to rely on the character of God to help you. If you are not reading your Bible, you won't know who God is and how much He cares about your heart in those hard times. Read the Bible every day.

- *This too shall pass.* Don't get caught in the panic of the moment. All hard times come and go.

- *While flowers love the sunshine, they also need the rain.* This season of hurt will pass—you will smile again. In the back of the clouds, the sun is always shining. And it will break through again.

7

Fitting In

It is not fitting, when one is in God's service, to
have a gloomy face or a chilling look.

—Saint Francis of Assisi

Ever been picked last at recess? Sat out on the bench? Worse yet, didn't make the team? The choir? Last chair in the band? The first one to be picked on or singled out in the crowd? Alone on the weekend? Not sure why you're here or what you're good at?

Come on...let's be honest. Do you know anybody who doesn't want to fit in? We all want to be chosen, to be needed for something or someone. We were created with this longing in our hearts. And it's ultimately God who fulfills it.

Paul said, "In him we were also chosen...in order that we...might be for the praise of his glory" (Ephesians 1:11-12). You were chosen by God to bring Him glory. You are God's servant! He says, "I have chosen you and have not rejected you" (Isaiah 41:9).

But as refreshing as that sounds, I sometimes wonder why it doesn't always feel like God chose me. Why would He choose *me* to bring Him glory? Have you ever felt that way?

When you feel like a misfit, it's as if everything and everybody around you has more power. More worth. You certainly don't feel like God would choose a misfit to represent Him and radiate His glory.

Satan loves it when we feel this way. I think he uses this cheap tool because he wants us to feel like we mean nothing to God or anyone else. Why? Because when you're rejected, left alone, or just feel like nobody notices you, one of two things usually happens. And neither is healthy.

We get depressed thinking we really are nothing, or we work extra hard to gain the attention of others just to feel like we fit in. And neither is healthy because in both cases we exchange God's glory for our own. Our dreary mood or our attention seeking behaviors become more about us.

Either way we choose, we buy into the lie of the enemy and forget that we are chosen by God to be His servant. We sacrifice the glory of God within us to find acceptance and seek out the attention of others for our own self gain with gloomy faces and dazzling acts. And the enemy loves it.

Desperate for Attention

If I glorify myself, my glory means nothing.
–JESUS, FROM JOHN 8:54

You see them. They're all over school. All over the stations you watch. And all over the magazines you read. They even fill up your screen when you log onto the internet. They come in different shapes, sizes, hair colors, and backgrounds. Some are rich. Some are poor.

But in most cases, you feel one of two ways about them. Either you hate them or you pity them.

Britney Spears. Lindsay Lohan. Paris Hilton. The girl at "that" lunch table. You know her. If she's stepped on your toes, you probably can't stand her. If you see her from a distance, you may pity her. She's the one who will do whatever it takes to get attention.

And she comes in all varieties:

-*Drama Queen Diane* Everything that happens in her life is exaggerated and blown out of proportion. She's a drain to be around because everything that happens in her life is so overly complicated...and about her.

> *If you have made mistakes, even serious ones, there is*
> *always another chance for you. What we call failure*
> *is not the falling down but the staying down.*
> –MARY PICKFORD

-*Rachel the Rescuer* She appears to be a very helpful and caring person. When you're in trouble, she is there. But it's not long before everybody in the world knows your problem and who is helping you! Rescuing you really isn't about you...but about her.

-*Sara the Sick* Poor Sara. She is always sick. Sore throat. Headache. Just down and out. Tired all the time. And when attention turns away from her, oh wait, she's sick again. Everybody notices she is not well and often ask among themselves, "Is she really sick?" Maybe in the head. Her illness is always...about her.

-*Vicki the Victim* For Vicki it's everybody else's fault. She is kind of like Eeyore (remember Winnie the Pooh?). You may find her moping around all of the time, but she mopes and complains because everybody is out to get her. She blames everybody else because she doesn't have a boyfriend. It's her dog's fault that she didn't get her homework done. Poor Vicki. It's always...about her.

-*Busy Brittany* "Oh my gosh. There is so much going on in my life!" This is all you hear about. How busy Brittany is. She never has enough time to do anything, except talk about how busy she is. It's always...about her.

They are the girls who have bought into the lie of the enemy— that they're worthless and not chosen. That God really doesn't care about them. So they go to all extremes to gain the validation, affirmation, and acceptance of other people. They seek to bring glory to themselves. And that's what Satan wants. He wants you to glorify yourself. Because when you do, you take it from God. But when we live to bring God glory through our actions, words, behavior, and faith, we steer clear of becoming one of these self-serving characters. Let's face it...we all probably fall into these behaviors now and then, but when we are aware of what to watch for, we can change those behaviors. When you find yourself throwing a pity party, take a sec to consider those in your life who are facing a harder situation. Stop the party of one...and lift up prayers for that person or family or situation. Your heart perspective will change in a flash. Then you can resume the party—just make it one of praise!

> *When we begin to take our failures non-seriously, it*
> *means we are ceasing to be afraid of them. It is of*
> *immense importance to learn to laugh at ourselves.*
> –KATHERINE MANSFIELD

Fitting In or Standing Out?

> *Always be a first-rate version of yourself, instead*
> *of a second-rate version of somebody else.*
> –JUDY GARLAND

One of the most amazing experiences of my life happened during my junior year. I was chosen to be one of five candidates on the Winterfest court. Winterfest is similar to homecoming, except five juniors are chosen and crowned at halftime of a basketball game instead of a football game. The day before the crowning, each contestant delivers a challenge to the student body.

I'll never forget the night I prepared the speech. It was a special moment with my mom because she was in the middle of writing her first book about discovering God's dream for your life. (Her book is called *Extraordinary Women: Discovering the Dream God Created for You*.) I was cuddling with Mom on the couch when we started talking about God's dreams for our lives. We discussed His plans versus our desires, His love versus our mistakes. As we talked, God challenged my own heart regarding a devotional I read just days before that...and I needed to know her thoughts.

So I asked her, "Why do we try so hard to fit in when God created us to stand out?"

As we fumbled around trying to answer the question, I began to realize the ways I strive to fit in. I felt bad, especially when my mom quoted Jesus. The least she could do was quote somebody I could disagree with.

She illustrated for me the story in John 8 when the Jews were asking Jesus who He was and making accusations about Him. Even accusing Him of being demon-possessed! This is when Jesus stood up for Himself and boldly made the claims about who He was, "I am not seeking glory for myself; but there is one who seeks it, and he is the judge" (John 8:50).

My mom said that Jesus knew He was created to stand out and not about to back down to the ridicule of others. He was so bold that the Jews picked up stones and were ready to kill Him right there in the temple! But Jesus hid from them and then quickly snuck out.

Jesus was, as Judy Garland describes, a first-rate version of Himself. He wasn't going to say He was somebody else to please the crowd. And He knew that this life wasn't about His own glory, but His Father's. Jesus wasn't created to fit in. And neither were you!

Think about this question for a moment, "Why do we try so hard to fit in when God created us to stand out?" Think about how much you try to fit in at school with the "in" crowd, with people you like. Or maybe you're working so hard to fit in with people you really don't know but think are "cool." They have the latest gadgets and toys. They are the stars on the sports teams. They make the grades. Or maybe they smoke. Even drink. You're not sure it's right, but they're at the parties you want to be invited to. People like them. Whatever it is—they're popular. They have everything you think you want.

Or so it seems.

> Our deepest fear is not that we are inadequate. Our deepest fear is that we are powerful beyond measure. It is our light, not our darkness that most frightens us. We ask ourselves, who am I to be brilliant, gorgeous, talented, fabulous? Actually, who are you not to be? You are a child of God. Your playing small does not serve the world. There is nothing enlightened about shrinking so that other people won't feel insecure around you. We are all meant to shine, as children do. We were born to make manifest the glory of God that is within us. It's not just in some of us; it's in everyone. And as we let our own light shine, we unconsciously give other people permission to do the same. As we are liberated from our own fear, our presence automatically liberates others.
>
> –from Nelson Mandela's inauguration speech

Journal Entry

Today was one of the most amazing days of my life! I gave my speech today as a Winterfest candidate and I watched Christ work through my life! It was amazing. Incredible. Exhilarating! It doesn't even matter who wins because I believe God allowed me to do this to show me I am capable of public speaking. The thing that touched me most was how many people told me they voted for me—not because *they did, but* why *they did. I want my* testimony to shine before everyone! I love you, Lord! I am yours now and forever! Thank you for blessing me today.

Love,
Your Princess Megan

Your Big Brother's Thoughts on...
Fitting In

Megan,

Do you ever lie in bed at night, restless as if something in your heart is longing for more? I do. Sure, we know we're loved by our family and friends. We even have more than we need—shelter, food, toys—and the list goes on.

Yet the more I get, the more I realize that I'm not satisfied. Something's missing.

I love this feeling because I know that God placed this emptiness into my heart. It is a longing to never be satisfied with this life, and He placed it there for one reason—to remind us that we don't belong here. We weren't created for earth.

My favorite band, Switchfoot, is lyrically brilliant. In their song "A Beautiful Letdown," they sing about their desire to fit in...until they realize they aren't supposed to. Not in this world. We don't belong to this place where we try so desperately to fit...we belong to God. That's the beauty of it.

Even the giants of the faith knew it. Abraham. Isaac. Jacob. Abel. Noah. Enoch. Even Rahab. They understood it. And were commended for it. But they only did so because "they admitted that they were aliens and strangers on earth. Instead, they were longing for a better country—a heavenly one" (Hebrews 11:13,16).

They knew they didn't belong here. And their faith in something more allowed them to do great things for God. They saw the value of heaven and were willing to pay a price for it.

Did they fit in here on earth? Hardly ever.

In heaven? I'm confident they are rejoicing even now.

Carry the cross and sing a song,
Josh

What's a Girl To Do?

> *If you belonged to the world, it would love you as its own.*
> *As it is, you do not belong to the world, but I have chosen*
> *you out of the world. That is why the world hates you.*
> JOHN 15:19

- *You were created to stand out for God.* Remember, you're only on this earth for a little while. Our time here comes and goes, but how you live and what you do here echoes in eternity. If you want to stand out in heaven...glorify Him on earth.

- *Challenge negative thinking.* Anytime you think someone else is cooler or more popular than you or you're worthless because you don't fit in where you want to, change your thoughts and focus on where God has you. Learn to have an attitude of gratitude and be thankful for the things God has done in your life. Your thankful heart will be contagious, and others will begin to follow you!

- *You have skills...find your strengths.* Learn to focus less on what you can't do and more on what you can do well. Tell yourself, "I can do all things...God does give me the power over sin. I have the freedom to choose whether I am going to screw around and blow everything or make the most of every opportunity for His glory. I choose to be happy today. To praise Him in the storm."

- *If you fail, pick yourself up and dust yourself off.* Learn from it and move on. I am learning that great people of God learned from their mistakes and chose new paths to success. They didn't quit.

- *Embrace your relationship with God.* Read the Word. Scripture reminds you that you are God's child, and there is a reason you're here. Believe and have faith that God wants to do big things with your life. Because He does.

Journal Entry

I've been thinking a lot lately about what God has planned for my future. I don't want to tell Him what I want to do. I want Him to tell me what He wants me to do. I was thinking about and marveling at how creative God is. We all have characteristics like His. How amazing! I resemble my Father! He looks at me with joy and beauty! I want to reflect His love!

Megan

> *Keep working hard and you can get anything that you want. If God gave you the talent, you should go for it. But don't think it's going to be easy. It's hard!*
> —Aaliyah

Listening to Dad

- *Failing at something is different than being a failure.* It took me a while to understand this. I hope you learn early that there is a big difference between the two.

- *Reach.* If you want to be successful, set goals, work hard, and reach for the stars. Nothing ventured—nothing gained.

- *Radiate His glory.* God has created you to shine for Him. I hope you know how much I love you. But know this—He loves you more. When you radiate His glory, you will be blessed. Free.

- *Stay focused on family and friends.* Love deeply. Laugh a lot—especially at yourself. And stay close to those you love. In the end, all that really matters is who you loved and who loved you.

8

Choices, Decisions, Consequences

Our very lives are fashioned by choice.
First we make choices. Then our choices make us.
—ANNE FRANK

I t's not shoes. It's not clothes. And it's not money. Though part of me wishes it were! There is one thing God gives you every single day. And He just doesn't give it to you one time each day. He gives it to you over and over again, every day you live. He will continue to give it to you for the rest of your life. Know what it is?

The ability to choose.

You are making a choice, even now, to read this book. You just chose to read this sentence. Whether or not you finish this book is your choice. To recommend it to a friend is your choice. There is probably something going on tonight that you are going to choose or not choose to attend. Doing your homework is a choice. Not doing your homework is a choice. Catch this: You cannot *not* choose. Not choosing to do something is still a choice.

I hate making decisions! After church it is the worst! Every Sunday, as soon as church lets out, there is family tension. Yeah, right after church! It's crazy. Nobody can ever decide on where we are going to eat. Everyone knows where they *don't* want to eat, but no one knows where they want to eat! Usually Dad will choose, and we'll just all go along with his decision. But sometimes he will purposely not choose. It makes me crazy because when he doesn't make a decision, nobody else can either. Including me.

Think about that for a moment. Even such a small thing as choosing a restaurant is so hard for many people. Especially girls—at least the girls I hang out with. I think it is because we are afraid of presenting an idea and having it shot down or laughed at. There's that confidence problem causing trouble again.

I'll never forget the time one of my guy friends told me about a date he went on. He took the girl out to an area of town with many restaurants and said to her, "Okay, you choose. Where do you want to eat?" He said she froze dead in her tracks and immediately went from talking his ear off to clamming up and st-st-ut-ut-uttering. She became more anxious with each passing moment.

Why is that? Why can't we make decisions?

Would Someone Please Make a Decision!

> *Successful people make their decisions quickly and*
> *change their minds slowly. Failures make their*
> *decisions slowly and change their minds quickly.*
>
> –Andy Andrews

As I journey through this thing we call life, I am finding out how hard it really is to make decisions. There are so many things that go into it. First, what if I make the wrong decision? Or what if my decision hurts somebody else? What if my boyfriend breaks up with me because of this decision? What will my parents think about this decision? Ugh! Making decisions can be so stupid and overwhelming.

On top of that, we have to fight our own inner battles. I'll admit it—I hate to fail. But more importantly, I hate to fail others. When my dad gave me that promise ring, and I vowed to stay a virgin until I was married, I certainly meant it. The one thing that keeps me from doing wrong in most situations is the fear that I will disappoint my mom and dad. I think this is a good fear though. I wish I would think more about how I disappoint God. Sometimes I forget how God might feel about my choices.

I think bad fears are different. Bad fears hold us back from making a decision at all. And as I said earlier, not making a decision is also making a decision. There are consequences either way. Many times I fear making a decision because I am unsure of myself. I am not confident that I have the courage or the wisdom to make the proper decision. I mean it feels good to grow up, but it's scary too. I hate the pressure of not knowing what I want to do when I grow up. My parents are successful, and I want to be successful too, but I fear failing. I just want to be successful in what God is calling *me* to be.

I have also found that there will always be people who laugh at you and try to knock you down. Girls can be so brutal—so mean to each other. But *you* can choose whether or not to listen to them. If you want those critics to have power over you, listen to them. If you want power over them, choose not to listen to their wasted breath.

I am not saying you shouldn't listen to constructive feedback from those who are smarter and wiser than you. You should! I'm simply saying that we cannot allow the criticism and bad talk of others to stop us from becoming and doing what God is calling us to be.

We have to stop doubting ourselves and just be confident in who we are. We must learn to make decisions and quickly move forward. If we hesitate too long and delay making the decision, we risk not making any decision at all. Self-doubt also causes us to question whether or not we made the right decision and be fearful of acting on any decision. Make a good decision. Act on it. And confidently get on with your life.

Choosing and Acting

We are always getting ready to live but never living.
–Ralph Waldo Emerson

There is a difference between choosing and acting. You make choices every day. The question is whether or not you act on the choices you make.

I have a friend who is overweight. She knows she weighs more than she should, and it affects the way she sees herself. A sweet and fun-loving girl, everybody at school adores her. But her weight makes her secretly unhappy, keeping her at home, away from hanging out with friends and going places.

I wish I had a dollar for every time she has vowed to start dieting and exercising. I would not have to worry about finding a career path. I'd be rich. Over and over again, she tells me and our closest friends how "this is her week," how she will "finally lose weight and feel good." She has gone as far as buying a new workout wardrobe and healthy foods. Yet it never seems to last more than a week. She is getting ready to live...but never living.

What about you? What about your New Year's resolutions? How many have you ever stuck to? A case of getting ready to live...but never living.

There are a lot of college graduates who return home to live with their parents. They have a college degree and work as a cashier. No goals. No direction. Some say they are never going to read another book again. And that's a big mistake. They got ready to live...but are not living.

Resolutions aren't just made or broken at the start of each new year. Nearly every day we set goals and do not follow through. It's like when I *chose* to read through the entire Bible in one year and failed miserably. I chose to read through the Bible, but didn't *act* on it. We make the choice, but have little to show for it. Or...the choices we are making are sucking the very life right out of us.

I often hear my dad quote the famous line from the movie *Braveheart:* "Every man dies. Not every man really lives." I want to live.

Choosing How to Live

> *God asks no man whether he will accept life. That is not*
> *the choice. You must take it. The only choice is how.*
>
> −HENRY WARD BEECHER

I am learning that there's a difference between getting ready to live and living. The difference lies in the choices we make. And those choices determine how we live.

As I look at my friends at school, I realize that some people make choices on their own, but more people make choices based on the responses of others. They are followers, not leaders.

I know a girl who says she has values, but if she were offered a drink of alcohol, she would probably take it just because she might think it is the "cool" thing to do. Because she wants to fit in with the people who drink. If a boy pushed her just a little, she would likely give in to sex. I just know it. She has no sense of who she is because her decisions are based on how she thinks others see her. She longs to fit in. She longs for them to like her. We all do.

I want people to like me. But if I compromise what I believe and what I stand for just because I want others to accept me, I've sacrificed all that I am. For those who don't know who they are, they're likely to make choices they'll forever regret.

I know a very brilliant girl who is a great example of this. I am talking top-ten-of-her-class-brilliant. Her family is very involved in church. She is a lot of fun and nice to everybody. She had a great reputation for being godly and leading others closer to the Lord.

Then she got involved in sex. Drinking. Partying. Pretty soon the entire school knew about it. It ruined her reputation. She gave in to the pressure and is now making choices that will forever haunt her. Your reputation is probably one of the hardest things to ever get back. Knowing yourself and what you stand for, I believe, is the first step to not falling into such decisions.

- Compared to teens with no sexually active friends, teens who report that half or more of their friends are sexually active are more than six and one-half times likelier to drink; 31 times likelier to get drunk; 22.5 times likelier to have tried marijuana; and more than five and one-half times likelier to smoke.

- Teens who attend religious services weekly are at less than half the risk of smoking, drinking or using illegal drugs as teens who do not attend such services.[1]

For a while, I was more consumed by my desire to have a boyfriend than anything else. I watched my friends pair off and have relationships. My friends' friends were in relationships. I would walk into Starbucks for coffee and who was in front of me? A couple loving on each other. I was always the third or fifth wheel when we went to the movies. And when we got inside, the couple in front of us was all lovey-dovey too! Ugh! I couldn't get away from it. I started feeling sorry for myself.

Only because I knew who I was in Christ did I get through that period of time without giving in to or settling on something I knew I would regret. My heart's desire was to be in a relationship. That was okay. The problem was that I placed that longing before my desire for God. When we do that, we do stupid things we swear we would never do!

Who You Are in Christ

Charm can mislead and beauty soon fades. The woman to be admired and praised is the woman who lives in the Fear-of-God.
PROVERBS 31:30 MSG

❦

Oh yes, you shaped me first inside, then out;
you formed me in my mother's womb.

PSALM 139:13 MSG

❀

It's in Christ that we find out who we are and what we are
living for. Long before we first heard of Christ and got our hopes
up, he had his eye on us, had designs on us for glorious living,
part of the overall purpose he is working out in everything and
everyone. It's in Christ that you, once you heard the truth and
believed it (this Message of your salvation), found yourselves
home free—signed, sealed, and delivered by the Holy Spirit.

EPHESIANS 1:11-13 MSG

Choices to Make Because of Who You Are in Christ

You did not choose me, but I chose you and appointed
you to go and bear fruit—fruit that will last. Then
the Father will give you whatever you ask in my
name. This is my command: Love each other.

JOHN 15:16-17

❀

Let the peace of Christ rule in your hearts...and be thankful.

COLOSSIANS 3:15

❀

Whatever you do, work at it with all your heart,
as working for the Lord, not for men.

COLOSSIANS 3:23

Knowing Yourself, Respecting Yourself, and Choosing the Right Way

> *Be careful how and what you choose. Minor choices*
> *in daily routines of living become guiding principles*
> *that later govern our thinking and actions.*
>
> —ANONYMOUS

It was one of those situations where a guy turns off the thinking bulb in his brain. Yeah, my boyfriend hung out with this girl, not realizing that he would rip my heart out by doing it. I felt intimidated by her. She is prettier than me. Flirtier than me. Older than me. And every boy was interested in her, including my boyfriend prior to our relationship!

I hate to see others hurt. In fact, I used to allow others to hurt me and wouldn't say anything about it to them because I didn't want the situation to blow up and cause them to hurt too.

Until the day the older, prettier girl stepped on my toes (and my pride)!

But just as I was practicing my boxing moves and considering being bold enough to take on the older, prettier girl, something hit me. There she was in my house...Bam! Whack! No, wait. Just kidding.

What did hit me that day was my need to take a step back and look at what was really happening in this situation. In a lot of ways, I was hurt by what happened. Okay, in every way I was hurt by what happened. But instead of pulling out the boxing gloves, I pulled out the tissues.

After I shed a few tears, I knew I couldn't be the nice little Megan who sweeps everything under the rug. I had to respect myself. I had to choose to confront my boyfriend and tell him how I was feeling... even though it might cost me the relationship. So I did what any smart, young, promising, (slightly jealous) girl would do—I helped him replace the thinking bulb in his really thick skull!

I walked into school and just looked at him with my sad, angry eyes. He looked at me and said, "What's wrong?"

I said, "Don't you know? Just think about it." Then I walked away. I was sick to my stomach. I just wanted to forget it all happened, but I knew I couldn't ignore it. Even if my boyfriend didn't mean anything by paying attention to this other girl, I didn't want to make excuses for him while ignoring my own feelings. Later that day we talked and I told him exactly how I felt. I made the choice to stand up for myself. I am Megan. I have a heart. I guard it closely. I make decisions that sustain who I am in Christ.

This experience wasn't life or death. It wasn't even a huge drama. But it was one that I might've walked away from just a year ago. I learned to not be afraid to confront others when they hurt me. It was also good for me because in the past my parents have been the ones to stand up for me in many situations. This experience taught me that I had to begin standing up for myself. Now when my boyfriend needs that thinking bulb changed, I tell him.

Your Big Brother's Thoughts on...
Knowing God

Megan,

You are doing great! I can tell by the journal entries you've shared that you are longing for more...genuinely seeking God in all that you do. Keep it up. I'm very proud of you!

I know it's not always easy. I struggle to get in the Word every day myself. It takes discipline, but it is worth it. Want to make good choices? The Bible is your guide. Choosing to read your Bible, though, is not just about finding out what is right and wrong. Most importantly it is about developing a personal, intimate relationship with God. Think about this. Do you have a relative—maybe a cousin—who you don't really know all that well? It's a relationship you would like to have but physical distance or a busy schedule seems to keep you from calling one another. And in the back of your mind, you know that you have to make the call because to have the relationship, you're the one who will have to make it happen. I think we all have relationships like this.

Especially with God.

You want to talk to Him. You want to hang out with Him. You want to get to know Him better. Yet you struggle to find the time. And when life gets tough, you get frustrated. And...you begin to feel that God is a long ways away—that's because He is (and guess who created the distance...not God!).

We get to a place where it's like we don't even know Him. That's because we don't.

What I've come to learn about my relationship with God is that I am 100 percent responsible for where I am in my walk with Him. He's always there waiting for me. But it's up to me to choose to respond.

Why does He feel distant? Because I chose not to call to Him in prayer. Why don't I feel like I know Him? Because I chose not to read His Word.

You determine where you go in your walk with God. You know right now whether or not you are close to Him. Is it time to call Him more often?

Choose every day to pray. Choose every day to read the Bible. And the choices you need to make in life will come much easier.

Growing in Him,
Josh

What's a Girl To Do?

You are who you spend time with.

−MY DAD

- *Make decisions based on the Word of God.* We need to be reading God's Word every day! If you're not, make a decision to read it daily for at least 30 minutes. And act on it! It will change your life, and decisions will no longer be as complicated as you might think.

- *The choices you make depend a lot on who you hang with.* You can be a leader or a follower. When you know who you are and what you stand for, you won't hang with people who might compromise what you believe. Decide who you are, what and who you'll associate with, and spend time with those who challenge you and build you up in Christ!

- *Don't fear failure.* I have great news for you—you will fail! You will lose. You will be hurt by others. Choosing not to enter into relationships or not to do things because you fear it may not work out the way you want it to will cripple you. You will get stuck in life because you will learn to never make decisions. Worst yet...you'll be lonely.

- *Choose to compliment people.* And be sincere about it. The more you serve others and make them feel good, the better you'll feel, the better you'll get to know them, and the less likely you'll be obsessed with yourself.

In darkness there is no choice. It is light that enables us to see the differences between things; and it is Christ who gives us light.
−JULIUS CHARLES HARE AND AUGUSTUS WILLIAM HARE

- *Respect yourself.* Don't sweep things under the rug. Know who you are in Christ and make decisions based on that.

One last thought. The other day we went to church. My mom made Zach wear a sweater that Santa brought him for Christmas. Zach hated it. He thought he looked silly—okay, he thought it was "girly."

As we were walking in, my "older brother," Josh, walked with Zach and told him the sweater looked good. Zach just looked at him with a face only Zach can make. Josh told him that it wasn't about the sweater. It was about who was wearing the sweater. He told Zach not to focus on how the sweater looked on him but to wear it proudly so that the other guys would want to wear it too...not because it looked good or bad, but because he was confident in it.

You see? You can choose. Does the sweater make you or do you make the sweater?

When you are the one making the decisions, you won't allow the sweater, other people, or what other people think make the decisions for you. You won't give in to things you said you never would just to "feel" good in the moment.

> *Always plan ahead. It wasn't raining when Noah built the ark.*
> –RICHARD CUSHING

Listening to Dad

- *Remember you always have a choice.* Choose wisely (James 1:13-18).

- *God wants you to live differently—His way.* When you do that, you'll be blessed. The only way you can do that is by spending time with Him.

- *Doing right doesn't always feel right, but in the end, it is always right.* I promise you that you'll be happy that you *chose right.*

- *When you blow it (and you will), make it right.* Ask God for forgiveness (1 John 1:9). Sure there will be *consequences*, but God loves to forgive and get you started on a clean, new path. I love that about God.

- *When you don't know what to do—what decision to make— step back and take a breath.* Then ask God for wisdom and seek out the counsel of godly friends. I am confident you'll decide exactly what to do (James 1:5).

9

Relationships and Drama

Just as lotions and fragrance give sensual delight,
a sweet friendship refreshes the soul.
PROVERBS 27:9 MSG

Four 16-year-old girls, friends since birth and all going different places for the summer, never had been apart...until now. The only thing that kept them connected to one another was a pair of jeans. Magical jeans.

Sound familiar? When I sat down to write this chapter, I immediately thought of the book series and movie titled *The Sisterhood of the Traveling Pants*. I couldn't think of a better illustration than the friendships shared between the four characters created by author Ann Brashares. The story is a great one because it is very likely that you can relate to one of the four characters.

The story unfolds when these friends are out shopping together before their summer break, and they find these great jeans. The wild thing is that the jeans fit all four of them perfectly even though they are all different heights and weights and body types! Upon this discovery they decide to share the jeans. Each girl will wear the jeans for one week and then mail them to the next friend with a note inside explaining what happened—good or bad—while they were wearing the jeans. This is how they decide to stay connected over the summer.

The first girl, Lena, goes to Greece. Afraid of falling in love, she doesn't like to look attractive or sexy. Staying conservative, she covers herself head to toe—her dresses flow to her ankles, and she is certain to show no cleavage. Though she comes from a loving family, she isn't sure anybody could love her. Lena's not even sure she can love herself. Fear cripples her ability to love.

The next girl, Bridget, is a gorgeous, blonde, athletic soccer player whose mom committed suicide when Bridget was in high school. Trying to find fulfillment in life, Bridget completely over-commits herself—and always looks for the hookup. When she goes away to a soccer camp for the summer, she is smitten with a cute coach. With a driven personality, her motto is "when I want something, I get it." This attitude leads her to make a decision she later regrets.

The third girl, Carmen, is Puerto Rican. Her dad, who is white, left her mom when Carmen was young, and though she never really forgave her dad, she still loves him. Because of that, she decides to spend the summer living with her dad. When she arrives, she finds out he is engaged and about to marry a woman with two kids. What she witnesses devastates her. To top it all off, the dress they order for Carmen to wear for the wedding is way too small. Feeling fat and horrible because it doesn't fit, she sits alone at the wedding reception. Carmen's anger gets the best of her when she realizes that nobody even comes looking for her. Desperate for her dad to notice her, she throws a rock through a window while everybody is eating. The trip is a complete disaster.

Finally there's Tibby, a rebellious girl with a streak of purple hair. She pretty much always has a negative vibe about her. She is sarcastic and moody. But she is also talented and creative and searching for a way to follow her passion to produce a documentary. Her independent streak means that she doesn't care what others think about her, but her attitude also keeps her from connecting with people except for this small circle of friends.

Crippled by Relationships

*I don't have time for superficial friends. I suppose
if you're really lonely you can call a superficial
friend, but otherwise, what's the point?*

–Courtney Cox, actress

Four girls. Four different worlds. Each has crippled and broken relationships. Scared, mad, sad, empty. These girls are all desperate for relationships and all that happens is pure drama, which follows them around wherever they go.

If you haven't seen the movie, you're probably wondering what happens? If you have, you can see if you agree with my "Megan's two-minute conclusion," my explanation of what I think is crippling their relationships.

First, Lena the timid girl. She grows a lot during her trip. She discovers that she really is lovable when a man she meets from Greece pursues her—and they fall in love. But it takes her a while to realize her worth and beauty.

I see a lot of girls like Lena. She sees that other people are worthy of being loved, but she isn't sure anyone could love her. All Lena sees are her flaws and someone not worthy to be loved. Looking down on yourself cripples not only your ability to love others, but it's also like telling God you're not happy with the way He created you—that He created somebody not worthy of love. The Bible says Jesus loves all of us and that He died for all of us (1 John 4:10).

When Bridget sends the pants to the next friend, she confesses to having sex and that it didn't make her feel like she thought it would. Bridget was looking to sex for fulfillment, but it couldn't fill the void in her heart. It made her depressed. That's when she started missing her mom. When she got home from her soccer camp, her friends came over to offer their support and convince her she didn't need to go down the same road as her mom and commit suicide over this. They were there for her even though she made mistakes.

Carmen is also like a lot of other girls. Angry. Ticked off at the world. And everybody around her knows it. When Carmen gets home, she realizes that she treats her friends, those she loves the most, like dirt. Yet she couldn't stand up to her dad. "Why is it that I can be mean to you (my friends), but I can't say these things to my dad, and he is the one I am angry at?"

One friend replies, "It's because you know we will always love you."

> *It is always easier to go with the crowd than to*
> *battle your way against it. It is always easier to*
> *conform than to be a nonconformist.*
> –WILLIAM BARCLAY

Doesn't that seem to always be the case? We can't stand up the person we're most angry with, yet we take it out on those we love the most. That's because I believe we attack those who we consider the safest—those who we know will be there for us through thick and thin. That's why it's easy to snap at our parents or siblings for something they didn't even do. We're letting our anger out but potentially hurting those we love. We have to be careful.

Finally there's Tibby. Even though she looked like she had it together and knew who she was, underneath the surface it was all a cover-up. She really had no idea. She was also scared to let anybody get close. To me she was the opposite of Lena. Tibby thought she was lovable and worthy to receive love from others but didn't believe she could trust other people to give her the love she needed. So instead of allowing others to love her, she put on a persona, a mask that prevented people from really getting to know her. When Tibby meets a young girl who has leukemia and still has a great attitude about life, Tibby's heart starts to change. This young girl's great attitude of hope, even though she is sick, helps Tibby appreciate people and life more than ever.

Can you relate to one of these girls? I know I can. In some ways, I can relate to all of them. Our lives are filled with choices, complications, relationships, and emotions. If we look back on these characters and imagine what we would do in each of their circumstances, we can learn a lot about ourselves. How would your faith impact each of the scenarios in the story? How does your faith impact your relationships?

What Color Are Your Eyes?

> *A friend is someone who knows the song in your heart, and*
> *can sing it back to you when you have forgotten the words.*
> –AUTHOR UNKNOWN

I believe you can tell a lot about a girl and the quality of her relationships just by looking into her eyes. Sad eyes. Angry eyes. Confused eyes. Crazy-in-love eyes. Scared eyes. Lonely eyes. And the ones I love the most, joyful eyes.

Read the following descriptions. What do people see when they look into your eyes?

Sad eyes. These girls have most likely been hurt by others. They just look sad. Even lonely. They mope around. And after hanging out with them, even you're sad. But this is how they live. I see some girls with sad eyes who know how to use them to make others interact with them—even pity them. Their sad eyes bring them attention.

❦

Angry eyes. Know anybody who uses her anger to manipulate other people to do things for her or make her happy? These girls use their anger to get attention. They are always ticked off at somebody.

And if you try to stay clear of them, they get upset at you for avoiding them.

❈

Confused eyes. These girls have no idea who they are or where they fit in the world. They're lost puppies. They often seem to be walking around in a state of confusion—getting caught up in things they shouldn't because they're not sure which road to take. And because the road with the least resistance is the easiest, they take it. But it's not long before they regret their decision. They get hurt. In trouble. And in many cases, they wander deeper into the pain and confusion. The cycle keeps going so they look to someone or something—anyone or anything—to help them find meaning in life. This often leads them in the wrong direction.

❈

Crazy-in-love eyes. These girls know they are beautiful. Pretty. And adored by the boys. Many describe her as airheaded. No depth. She talks but nobody listens. She is the stereotypical blonde though she may not even be blonde. She is in and out of relationships with guys who are hot—and only with them because they are hot. When he is tired of her, he dumps her. She is hurt over and over again. But very soon along comes—you guessed it—love once again.

❈

Scared eyes. Timid. Fearful. She loves the attention of others, but when it comes to commitment, she avoids it by saying she wasn't interested anyway. Afraid of being hurt, she only allows others to get so close. Her relationships remain superficial because she won't let anybody in. Her inner beauty stays hidden. She never lets others know the real her.

❈

Lonely eyes. I think all of the eyes I just described fit into this category. Many girls are lonely. They have nobody to talk to. They lie in bed at night wondering if anybody really cares, if anybody is really there for them, and if anybody really understands. This is a sad thing. We weren't created to be alone. Yet so many of the girls I see today are just that—in a crowd, but all alone.

❀

Joyful eyes. I am not talking about the googly-eyed girl who seems to force her smile (no matter what happens). I'm talking about the girl who truly walks around with the joy of Christ in her eyes. You can see the joy in her. And it doesn't matter what she is going through. She may be sad, but you can see the joy in her heart. She may be angry, but she knows how to handle it. She truly cares about other people. And other people want to drink from her joy, her beauty, and her freedom. The girl with joyful eyes is alive!

The Nasty Part of Relationships—Conflict

> *Only your real friends will tell you when your face is dirty.*
> –Sicilian Proverb

I'll bet ya my favorite jeans that 100 percent of the readers of this book are human! And because you are human, you will have conflicts. It's inevitable. Most girls I know, including myself, hate conflict. But let me tell you, conflict does not have to mean drama. Think of a time you had a major blowup with a friend and you worked through it together. At the end of the conflict, didn't you feel closer to one another? It's like you needed the conflict to get to a new stage in your relationship. I think that's because conflict builds intimacy in relationships. We need to go through the fire before we can forge a stronger bond.

The Bible says to live at peace with one another (Romans 12:18). When somebody hurts you or does you wrong, Jesus commands you to go to the person and show him or her their fault, just you and the other person (Matthew 18:15). It's biblical to confront somebody who has done you wrong.

> *My best friend is the one who brings out the best in me.*
> –HENRY FORD

John Ortberg, a really great pastor whose books I like to read, wrote about a model of how to seek reconciliation in a relationship. First, acknowledge that there is a conflict. Second, take responsibility for your part in the conflict. After that, take action. Go to the person and sit with them, one-on-one, alone. Don't involve other people. Explain clearly what she has done to hurt or offend you. You can describe what you experienced and observed, how it made you feel, the consequences of this behavior, and request that a change take place. Throughout the process be sure to check your motives. Remember, reconciliation is always the goal...not being in the right.[1] Dr. Ortberg says, "God commands us to forgive whenever we're hurt, and reconcile whenever we can, because life is too short not to do so."[2]

Whether it's with your parents, friends, siblings, or someone else who you are having conflict with, make sure you seek reconciliation with those who have hurt you. And if you have hurt somebody else, go to him or her and offer your apologies. I know it's not easy, but you'll be glad you did.

Do Relationships Matter?

> *The real test of friendship is: Can you literally do nothing with the other person? Can you enjoy together those moments of life*

that are utterly simple? They are the moments people look back
on at the end of life and number as their most sacred experiences.
–EUGENE KENNEDY

I know I've talked a lot about relationships in this book. But that's because I believe they're the most important thing in life. It's what God created us for.

Lying in bed at night, what do you worry about the most? What do you think about? What are you longing for? Maybe you are so excited you can't sleep. No matter the context, my hunch is that your nighttime thoughts are filled with the relationships in your life, in some form or another. Boyfriend. Mom. Dad. Best friend. Sister. Brother. Grandparent. A coworker, classmate, or roommate. The lady you talked to at the grocery store who is going through chemotherapy for cancer. Your youth pastor. The little girl at church who clings to you every Sunday morning. An old friend. The people who sat at the table next to you at the restaurant the other day. I think you get the picture. Relationships are everywhere.

When we get to heaven I don't think God is going to care so much about whether or not we got an A or a B on our last math test. I do believe He will care about the people we've influenced during our time on earth. "Well done, good and faithful servant" will be said to us because of the good things we have done for others. What influence are you having on those around you? What do people say about the way you treat others? Are you a *real* friend?

The most beautiful discovery that true friends can make is
that they can grow separately without growing apart.
–ELIZABETH FOLEY

Your Big Brother's Thoughts on...
Life's Inconveniences

Megan,

Not too long ago I was sitting on an airplane beside a woman who appeared to be in her fifties. When the stewardess came by to offer a drink, the woman politely said, "Tomato juice." I ordered a Diet Coke and all was good. Until...

Just as the stewardess handed the woman her tomato juice, the airplane hit turbulence and a few drops—let me say that again, a few drops—of tomato juice spilled onto the woman's shirt. You would have thought the stewardess purposely dumped the entire can of juice all over the woman. She went berserk. Bonkers. She lashed out at the stewardess and made a huge scene. I couldn't believe it.

I began thinking about the people in this woman's life. What about her husband? I wouldn't want to be married to her. What about her kids? Heaven forbid they spill anything on the floor.

Isn't it amazing the stress we put ourselves through by allowing unimportant things to affect who we are and how we treat others? It affects our quality of life. And it affects those around us when we blow a fuse. It's contagious. Your overreaction will set off a stressful chain reaction. It makes you and those you're with look foolish.

But understand this: Who you are and how you respond in times of stress is who you really are in relationships. The next time you are under severe stress, ask yourself, "What are the fruits of the Spirit that I can apply here? How can I live in such a way that I don't struggle with making molehills into mountains?"

You need to understand this. Or you will jeopardize the relationships in your life.

Love you,
Josh

What's a Girl To Do?

In *The Sisterhood of the Traveling Pants,* you can see the importance of having friends who love you. Maybe you have a circle of friends right now just like this. If you are that fortunate, hang on to them. They need you. You need them.

If you've had a hard time connecting in relationships, it's time to make a commitment to discovering why. You need other people to help you through life. Getting into healthy relationships with people who love you unconditionally is the first step to finding freedom. Need to cut the drama?

- *Get into healthy relationships.* We need others. But we don't need others who drag us down and make us do things we don't want to do. Maybe you have been hurt by people who were supposed to have loved you. If so, you can't stay caught up in it. Blaming them for the hurt in your life will not help you break free. Getting into healthy relationships will. Make those connections. You need other people.

- *Learn to respond.* Our emotions are directly tied to our relationships. Look into the eyes of a girl long enough and you can tell if she is angry, sad, lonely, or confused. If she allows these emotions to guide her decisions in relationships, she is very likely to run into problems. As I said earlier in the book, we need to respond, not react.

Think of a first date. Do you kiss him because it feels good? A reactor would say, "Yeah, go for it!" A responder would say, "Don't give him that benefit. Guard your heart!" You cannot allow your actions to be based on how you feel in the moment.

Are your feelings about the relationship a little confusing? When relationships get sticky, take a step back and think through what may or may not be happening before you respond.

- *Discover your relational strengths.* We are all different. We all have to grow up and discover who we are. You don't have to change who you are to be confident. The truth is you have strengths inside of you that make you beautiful and unique. Too often, though, we focus only on our weaknesses. But know this: You *cannot not* have an influence in other people's lives. You are always influencing other people. The question is this: What is your influence? Are you helping or hurting others? Your lack of confidence will impact the lives of other people or your confidence will. Which do you want?

> *Do not follow where the path may lead. Go, instead, where there is no path and leave a trail.*
> —RALPH WALDO EMERSON

Listening to Dad

- *Your worth and value do not come from what others think about you.* Always be cautious and don't listen to them. Cherish who you are in Christ.

- *Remember, you always have a choice.* If the drama is too much, you need to step back and reevaluate your role as friend. Don't get caught up in their "stuff." Doing right doesn't always feel right, but in the end it is always right. Trust God's Word for direction so you know how to make good choices.

- *Learn to trust.* Will you get hurt? Yes (and it's these times that break my heart into pieces as your dad), but the hurt will only make you wiser and stronger in the end.

- *Be careful who you hang out with.* Who you associate with the most is who you become most like. Hang around people who "get it" and are *real*...not superficial and fake.

10

Totally His

*Jesus—God—had always wanted to be with me? God has
been lonesome for me? There was no condemnation in His voice,
no scolding, no list of rules—just the deepest of longings.*

–JULIE MILLER, SINGER

O ld. Ragged. Faded pink. Baby was worn out, but I didn't care. I
took her everywhere with me. To bed. To eat. To bath. Outside
to play. It never mattered if I had gotten a new doll for Christmas,
I still kept Baby right beside me.

Did you ever have a blankie? A stuffed animal? Or maybe a
doll you just couldn't bear to get rid of? That was me. I was the one
with the doll. I played with her all the time. Even though I would
get new toys for my birthday or Christmas, I could never give up
Baby. I cherished that ragged, old, worn-out pink doll. As the years
went on, my family made sure she came along with us wherever
we went. To this day, my mom still has Baby. For some reason she's
never been able to throw her away.

I forgot about Baby for a while, but then I read a story by John
Ortberg. Now I have a totally new understanding of Baby's significance and why my mom has yet to pitch her.

Dr. Ortberg tells of his sister's doll, Pandy. (Don't get confused.
John Ortberg's sister's name is Barbie—Pandy is the doll in the
story. Barbie is a real person.) Just like I did with my doll, Barbie
did everything with hers. She loved Pandy very much. But eventually Pandy got old. She lost an arm, most of her hair, and even her

stuffing. Gangly and barely held together, Pandy was still Barbie's favorite toy.

Dr. Ortberg remembers one year when he and his sister went on a trip to Canada, and as they were driving back, they realized that Pandy had been left behind at the hotel. What did they do? The family drove all the way back to Canada to get Pandy. They drove from Illinois!

Eventually Barbie grew up and Pandy was put on the shelf. (I love this part of the story.) John Ortberg writes that the doll was a mess and should have been thrown out, but his mom could never do it. Instead, she wrapped Pandy in tissue paper and put her in the attic.

Why not just throw the ragged old doll away? Why has my mom yet to throw Baby away? Dr. Ortberg explains that Pandy was worth saving because of Barbie's love for her. Barbie's love for the decrepit doll made it valuable—and worth keeping. Eventually they had Pandy restored. Finally everyone could see why Pandy was so beautiful.[1]

I love that. Because of my little-girl-love for Baby, my mom decided to keep her. It was my love for Baby that has made her valuable.

It's that way with God too. I am Pandy. You are Pandy. We are all Pandys. Broken. Worn-out at times. Old. (Okay, maybe not so much old.) But hurt by the wear and tear of life and those around us. We sin and are sinned against. There are some of you that probably think you would be better off thrown away. Stop thinking this way. You're wrong. Because God loves you—you're valuable! You are worth keeping!

God loves you so much that He sent His one and only Son to die for you. To save you. To be with Him in eternity. Jesus even prayed to the Father that you—yes, you—could be with Him. "Father, I want those you have given me to be with me where I am" (John

17:24). Good news, girls! "This is love: not that we loved God, but that he loved us and sent his Son" to save us (1 John 4:10). He wants to keep you. He takes care of you. He carries you everywhere with Him and will even come back to get you when you're lost. He loves you. Love conquers your sin. Love heals your bruises. Love overcomes your pain. Love reflects your beauty. Love increases your value.

Dr. Ortberg closed the story by saying, "There is such a love, a love that creates value in what is loved. There is a love that turns rag dolls into priceless treasures. There is a love that fastens itself onto ragged little creatures for reasons that no one could ever quite figure out, and makes them precious and valued beyond calculation. This is a love beyond reason. This is the love of God. This is the love with which God loves you and me."[2]

I love that about God!

An Intimate Love

God knows me intimately and loves me anyway.
–J.I. PACKER

Let's face it—being totally His is not easy. Oftentimes we lose focus of God and turn to other things to find significance and self-worth. To feel loved. Cherished. Beautiful. Connected. We want to belong and be intimately known.

Sometimes in our search for belonging we give too much of ourselves. In our longing for someone to know us—to intimately know us—we become obsessed with other people, other things, or even ourselves. We spend too much on clothes. Nails. Hair. Makeup. We place too much of our significance in our social standing at school. Hanging with the "popular" crowd is more important than being with genuinely good people who will really care about us. We find 24/7 boyfriends. And if we don't settle with one boyfriend, we keep many boy "friends" around to feed off of the attention they are paying us.

Don't misunderstand me. I'm not saying friends are bad. If you've read the first nine chapters, you know I think you need to have good friends. I'm also not saying that having nice clothes, makeup, and hair are bad. Or that boyfriends are bad. What I am saying is that these things are bad when we use them to feed the loneliness in our hearts or turn to them, instead of God, to find the intimacy and worth we so desire.

I've heard my dad say that you can tell a person's priorities in life by where they are spending their time. Think about that for a moment. What are you spending the most time doing? Who are you with the most? How much time are you spending in prayer? In the Bible?

Now make a list of the things you do that take up more time than you give to God. Save it because you'll need it later in the chapter.

Letting Go

> *A good friend is hard to find, hard to*
> *lose, and impossible to forget.*
> –Author Unknown

When my boyfriend was leaving town, I was faced with a truth— one I wrote about in the following journal entry. I'm not very good at goodbyes. Never have been. I guess I get pretty attached to anyone (or anything) that is important to me. Can you relate?

Journal Entry

Why is being alone so...lonely? I need to know my boyfriend loves me...and yet I do. How is that logical? How does that make sense? I feel like we are beginning this college separation. And just so you know—it's hard! He left yesterday. One of the hardest things I've ever done in my life was watch him get on that plane. No, the hardest thing was letting that plane leave. When I finally got home, my mom met me at the door, and for the first time that day, I broke down. It felt so good to have her cry with me...

Megan

When we were talking later that day, my mom said to me, "It's okay to cry. It shows how much you care." She told me that she and my brother knew letting my boyfriend go would be hard because letting go is something that has never been easy for me.

She recalled a story of when I was a little girl. I had a puppy named Rio, and for some reason, my dad would sometimes accidentally let him loose. Rio would run away as fast as he could, making it very hard to catch him. I would run after Rio, crying and screaming until my dad, after a fierce chase, would place him back into my arms.

After mom reminded me of my love for Rio, she said, "How could we expect you to be any different with a person?" I must say I hate change. I hate letting go most of all. But I'm telling you, there are things in life we have to let go of to become totally God's. Jesus said to gain life, we must lose it (Matthew 10:39). He said, "What kind of deal is it to get everything you want but lose yourself? What could you ever trade your soul for?" (Matthew 16:26 MSG). Even Paul said, "To live is Christ and to die is gain" (Philippians 1:21). We have to die to the idols in our lives. We have to stop placing other things, people, and ourselves before God. Give Him back His rightful place in our lives, that is complete control of our heart.

When I realized how lonely I was after my boyfriend left for college, I knew I had to turn back to God and give Him His rightful place in my heart.

Journal Entry

Lord,

Forgive me for feeling lonely because I know You are here and You have never left me alone. Thank You for Your consistency—for loving me yesterday, today, and always. Father, use me. Make me glad and joyful! I love You, holy Lord!

Love,

Megan

Your Life—His Dream

> *You never know God is all you need until God is all you have.*
> —RICK WARREN

God wants to give you His best. As the great American missionary Jim Elliot once said, "God always gives His best to those who leave the choice with Him." God knows your faithfulness and will reward you for it. He knows when you choose Him. I know how easy it is to sometimes lose heart thinking everybody else is out doing things while you sit there like Tweedledee or Tweedledum twirling your fingers and feeling as if you're missing out. God sees that. He knows how faithful you are. He loves that about you. I know it doesn't always seem like He cares what you're doing, but He does! The Bible says He rejoices in our righteousness.

That doesn't mean life is carefree and easy. People will let you down. Sometimes it'll even seem like God let you down. But He keeps bringing you back to center to find purpose, meaning, and value.

He knows your heart. He knows how hard you try to be like Him and want to be like Him. He knows your future. He knows your fears. He knows your follies and failures and loves you anyway.

I'm telling you—God wants you to have His best. He wants you to be totally His. But the choice is yours. God loves you so much He even gave you the freedom of whether or not to choose Him. Choose today to be totally His.

Your Big Brother's Thoughts on...
Don't Let Your "But" Get in the Way

Megan,

Did you ever stop to think about what it would be like to live forever and ever and ever with nothing in the universe but yourself? I have. And it's scary. So much so that I have now started a personal journey to discover what it means to live forever. Doing so has taken me to Ecclesiastes 3:11, "He has also set eternity in the hearts of men [and women]; yet they cannot fathom what God has done from beginning to end." I love that verse. The first time I read it, I wrote a little note at the top of my Bible that read, "How do we tap into the eternity that God has placed into our hearts?" Right underneath it I wrote, "Don't let your 'buts' get in the way."

What do I mean? Think about the things you say from time to time that prevent you from growing deeper in your relationship with Christ. We say things like, "I was going to go to that small group tonight, but I couldn't get a ride." "I was going to begin journaling today, but I figured I would wait because I have a paper to write and don't want to confuse myself." "I was going to go to church, but I haven't slept well in a while and needed to sleep in." "I was going to pray, but...but...but...but..."

As I process what it means to have eternity set in my heart, I reflect on the way I live my life. Why am I doing what I do? What motivates me? Am I living for Christ, or am I making excuses? Am I influenced more by what others think I should do, or do I have a true sense of who I am and what I'm doing? When I die, will Jesus put His hand on my back and say "Well done"?

Some folks don't even think about the eternal realm. I am not sure how people process life and find meaning in it without an understanding of what happens to them when they die. For many Christians, being saved is enough. They know what they believe, but I'm not sure they know why they believe. I find more admiration for those who follow other religions or no religion and have a clear understanding and deep conviction of why they believe that way than Christians who walk aimlessly through life with no recollection of why they believe what they do. And sadly enough, when we've lost the "why" in our lives, we've lost the passion for living. It always reflects back on our actions and the way we live.

If you can see beyond this life on earth and begin seeing the eternity that God has set in your heart, your life will be transformed. You will see things differently. Doing what's right will be easier than doing what feels good.

Don't make excuses and let your "buts" get in the way. Keep your heart set on eternity and always remind yourself what Maximus Aurelius in Gladiator *said: "What we do in life, echoes in eternity."*

Love you,
Josh

Accepting His Love

> *God loves each of us as if there were only one of us.*
> —SAINT AUGUSTINE

Read this next part aloud. If you're in a library or a place where you will distract other people, read it two or three times to yourself. I want you to understand this.

I am much more valuable than the birds of the air and the lilies of the field. Yet God feeds the birds and makes the lilies grow. Because I am much more valuable than they are, God will take care of me too. He loves me.

In fact, God even has the very hairs on my head numbered. He knows me. He knows my thoughts. He knows my actions. He is familiar with all my ways. I cannot flee from His presence. God is always with me. He loves me.

He created me from the beginning. He knit me together in my mother's womb. My frame was not hidden from Him. God recorded all the days of my life before one of them even came to be. God loves me. I am fearfully and wonderfully made. He loves me with an everlasting love.

Don't just read this last paragraph. Meditate on it. Have you accepted the love of the Father, who sent His Son Jesus to die for you? Have you accepted Jesus Christ as your personal Savior? Do you understand what He went through on the cross just for *you*? Read the following passages a few times too. They reflect God's heart and His love for you. He would do anything for you. Scratch that. He did do everything for you. Now you just need to accept Him and fall in love with Him like I did.

Don't be afraid, I've redeemed you.
I've called your name. You're mine.
When you're in over your head, I'll be there with you.
When you're in rough waters, you will not go down.
When you're between a rock and a hard place,
it won't be a dead end—
Because I am GOD, your personal God,
The Holy of Israel, your Savior.
I paid a huge price for you:
all of Egypt, with rich Cush and Seba thrown in!

That's how much you mean to me!
That's how much I love you!
I'd sell off the whole world to get you back,
trade the creation just for you.
Isaiah 43:1-4 MSG

❀

Your GOD is present among you,
a strong Warrior there to save you.
Happy to have you back, he'll calm you with his love
and delight you with his songs.
Zephaniah 3:17 MSG

Journal Entry

Wow, I was just flipping through this journal and looking at all the amazing things God has done for me—it's overwhelming! Today I need to make a commitment—no matter how crazy life gets I can't forget my Savior, my Love, my Beginning, my End, my Life! Abba, I love You! Help me show my love for You today and forever! Without You I am ordinary, and You have enough ordinary people here. With You I am so much more! Use me! Teach me! You never let me down! Thank you!

Love,

Megan

You and I are on the same journey in many ways. We'll experience some of the same trials, and yet there will be a lot of things we encounter that are unique. But what is so great about being sisters in faith is that we can lift one another up...even if we don't know each other.

I'm so excited for you and your journey. The following steps are what you can do to solidify your faith. Don't forget that you're never alone. We're in this together because we are both totally His. Isn't it great!

> *God loves us the way we are, but too much to leave us that way.*
> —LEIGHTON FORD

What's a Girl To Do?

- *Accept Him.* Do you know Jesus Christ as your personal Lord and Savior? If not, I encourage you to pray the following prayer to accept Him into your heart. It's the first step to becoming totally His.

> Father, I know I have sinned against You and I'm sorry. I am now ready to turn away from my sinful past and become a new creation in You. Please forgive me of my sins and begin Your work in me. I believe that Your Son, Jesus Christ, died for my sins, was resurrected from the dead, is alive, and hears my prayer even now. I invite Jesus to become the Lord of my life and to rule and reign in my heart. Please send Your Holy Spirit to help me obey You and to do Your will for the rest of my life. In Jesus' name I pray. Amen.

> You've always been God's girl. He chases you. If you said yes to Him and accepted Him as your Savior, you are always His. Being totally His is your choice. He is totally yours. Be totally His.

- *Find a great man or woman of God that you look up to and follow their example.* Learn from them. Watch them. Model their Christ-centered behaviors. Paul said to be followers of his example. If you can't find time to be with these faith models, call them. Write letters to them. Facebook them. Do something to be with somebody who will speak God's truth into your life. Search for it with all of your heart. I've said it a million times, "You are who you spend time with." Here is my journal entry below. In this one I wrote a letter to my grandpa.

Journal Entry

Today has been a hard day for me to accept. I just found out my Papa (my dad's dad) is dying...I want to write a letter to him instead of a regular journal entry.

Papa,

I love you so much! You were always someone I could look to as a godly example. I don't know why, but I don't believe you can die! Why does God take champions of this world out? Papa, you are a champion! If any man deserves a crown from Christ Himself, it is you! I know I might not be your closest granddaughter because I'm young, but whenever I am around you, you make me feel like your favorite. I remember when you baptized me...in that nasty creek water! I remember that strong fragrance of Old Spice when you first came out of the bathroom, your love of people, your prayers, your stories, your proud face when you saw me at Winterfest in my yellow dress, and especially how proud you were when you looked at my dad. I hope I marry a man like you—someone to lead me and our family closer to the heart of our Savior Jesus Christ.

If there's one thing you taught me, it was that Jesus reigns in our home forever! That He is all I need and all I could ever want! That He loves us and holds on to us when no one else can or will. I prayed for your healing, Papa, but if God decides that it's time for you to go home...wait for me and greet me in heaven. I hope I become like you.

All my love,

Megan

(My Papa died two days later.)

- *You've got to talk to somebody.* Keeping things bottled up inside only leads to trouble and more heartache. Talk it out with someone you trust!

- *Choose your influences wisely.* Read your Bible. Pick up some Christian books. Listen to worship songs. I love listening to worship music. It keeps me close to God. If you put garbage in, garbage will come out. Be careful what you watch on television, what radio station you listen to, and what magazines you read!

- *Don't quit.* Don't give up on your faith and your growth as a woman of God. Great things await you as a believer. Stay strong and the confidence will come. Surround yourself with people and things that remind you to serve the Lord so that you won't get discouraged.

- *Cut down on other priorities.* Earlier I said that you learn about your priorities in life by realizing where you spend the most time. Take that list you made of the things you do that take up more time than you give to God and shave off five minutes a day from each one. Just five minutes from each activity. That's all. Now take that extra time and begin using it to spend an extra 30 minutes a day reading the Bible, journaling, and praying to God. I love to go to bed 30 minutes earlier so that I can have that time with God right before I fall asleep at night. You may have another time that suits you better—but just make sure you are doing it. Remember, what you put in… it's what will come out. If you want people to know you are totally His, you have to reflect His character. And the only way to reflect His character is to spend time with Him getting to know His character. To know His character, you have to read His Word—every day.

Begin giving each of these six things to Him in prayer. And don't forget, most importantly, to spend time in the Bible and alone with God daily. Why don't you give Him everything right now! Pray.

Listening to Dad

- *Believe that God has a dream for you.* "'For I know the plans I have for you,' declares the LORD, 'plans to prosper you and not to harm you, plans to give you hope and a future. Then you will call upon me and come and pray to me, and I will listen to you'" (Jeremiah 29:11).

   When you were little, I dreamed of what you could and would be someday. But I know God's plan and His dream for you is all that matters. I can only imagine what He dreams for your life. Ask Him. Seek Him. Embrace Him. And then live the dream.

- *God loves you more!* While it is hard for me to believe, He loves you more than I do. You're His. You always have been. Draw your love and life from His. John 15:15 says, "that without [Him] you can do nothing."

- *You are who you spend time with.* I just have to reinforce this one more time! The more you put Him at the center of your life, the more strength and joy you will find in this life. Spend time with others who put Christ first, and you'll have support, encouragement, and inspiration.

- *Remember tough times don't last...tough people do.* A tough woman is a woman who is strong in the Lord. Psalm 1:1,3 promises, "Blessed is the man [or woman] who does not walk in the counsel of the wicked...He is like a tree planted by streams of water, which yields its fruit in season and whose leaf does not wither. Whatever he does prospers."

No matter the journey, honey, know that I love you and believe in you.

Love,
Dad

❀

There has never been the slightest doubt in my mind that the God who started this great work in you would keep at it and bring it to a flourishing finish on the very day Christ Jesus appears.
PHILIPPIANS 1:6 MSG

❀

I don't know where you're at or what you're going through, but I know this: God does. Becoming totally His is about a decision only you can make. And only you can keep. God loves you. You are totally His. Know that I am praying for you.

Love,
Megan

Notes

Chapter Two

1. "When wearing a swimsuit on the beach, you feel?" poll from April 2007 www.seven teen.com/fashion/swimsuit poll. Retrieved October 1, 2007.

2. "Did you know?" from http://www.dietjokes.co.uk/jokes/053.php. Retrieved December 10, 2007.

3. National Center for Chronic Disease Prevention and Health Promotion. 2005. Youth online: Dietary Behaviors. *From* http://apps.nccd.cdc.gov/yrbss/CategoryQuestions .asp?Cat=5&desc=Dietary%20Behaviors. Retrieved October 4, 2007.

4. National Eating Disorders Association. 2006. Statistics: Eating Disorders and Their Precursors. From http://www.nationaleatingdisorders.org/p. asp?WebPage_ ID=286&Profile_ID=41138.

5. F. Kuffel, "Size and Sensibility," *Psychology Today*. January-February 2005. From http://www.psychologytoday.com/articles/pto-3642. Retrieved October 1, 2007.

6. "Dieting among teens," *Eating Disorders Review*. November/December 2003.

7. Anorexia Nervosa and Related Eating Disorders, Inc. 2007. *Statistics: How many people have eating disorders?* From http://www.anred.com/stats.html. Retrieved September 26, 2007.

8. *He was only a chocolate chip cookie.* From http://www.dietjokes.co.uk. Retrieved December 10, 2007.

Chapter Three

1. D. Witmer, "Should parents set the age to start?" Teen dating poll. 2007. From http://parentingteens.about.com/gi/pages/poll.htm?linkback=http://parenting teens.about.com&poll_id=5024488571. Retrieved September 24, 2007.

2. N. Seiler, "Is teenage marriage a solution?" 2002. From http://www.clasp.org/publi cations/teenmariage02-20.pdf. Retrieved September 24, 2007.

Chapter Four

1. About poll: "Have you ever been in love?" 2007. From http://teenadvice.about.com. Retrieved October 1, 2007.

2. About poll: "Do you understand the difference between lust and love?" 2007. From http://teenadvice.about.com. Retrieved October 1, 2007.

3. M.M. Bersamin, D.A. Fisher, J.W. Grube, D.L. Hill, S. Walker. 2007. "Defining virginity and abstinence: Adolescent's interpretations of sexual behaviors." *Journal of Adolescent Health*, vol. 41 (2007), pp. 182-188.

4. About poll: "If you have had sex, do you wish your first time had been different or that you had waited?" 2007. http://teenadvice.about.com. Retrieved October 1, 2007.

5. Kaiser Family Foundation, "Sexual health knowledge, attitudes, and experiences. A series of national surveys of teens about sex," October 2003.

6. Kaiser Family Foundation, "Virginity and the first time: A series of national surveys of teens about sex," October 2003. From http://www.kff.org. Retrieved October 8, 2007.

Chapter Five

1. K.S. Berger. *The Developing Person Through the Life Span,* 6th ed. (New York: Worth Publishers), 2008.

2. D.P. Welsh, C.M. Grello, and M.S. Harper, "When love hurts: Depression and adolescent romantic relationships," quoted in Paul Florsheim, ed. *Adolescent Romantic Relations and Sexual Behavior: Theory, Research, and Practical Implications* (Mahwah, NJ: Lawrence Erlbaum Associates, Inc, 2003), pp. 185-212.

3. Ibid.

4. About Poll: "Are teens mature enough to really fall in love?" 2007. From http://teenadvice.about.com/gi/pages/poll.htm?poll_id=5829043553&linkback=http://teenadvice.about.com.

5. Neil Clark Warren, *Finding the Love of Your Life: Ten Principles for Choosing the Right Marriage Partner* (New York: Pocket Books, 1992), p. 16.

Chapter Six

1. K.S. Berger, *The Developing Person Through the Life Span*, 6th ed. (New York: Worth Publishers, 2005).

2. P.K. Trickett, D.A. Kurtz, and J.G. Noll. The Consequences of Child Sexual Abuse for Female Development, quoted in D.J. Bell, S.L. Foster, & E.J. Mash, eds., *Handbook of Behavioral and Emotional Problems in Girls* (New York: Plenum Publishers, 2005), pp. 357-80.

3. C.M. Buchanen. Girls Adjustment to Divorce and Remarriage," quoted in D.J. Bell, S.L. Foster, & E.J. Mash, eds., *Handbook of Behavioral and Emotional Problems in Girls.* (New York: Plenum Publishers, 2005), pp. 415-38.

4. According to the *American Psychiatric Association.* "Let's Talk Facts About Common Childhood Disorders." 2005. http://healthyminds.org/multimedia/commonchildhooddisorders.

5. National Fatherhood Initiative, "Father Facts" (3rd ed).

6. According to divorce statistics retrieved from http://www.divorcemag.com.

7. A. Andrews, *Mastering the Seven Decisions that Determine Personal Success* (Nashville, TN: Thomas Nelson Publishers, 2008), p. 19.

Chapter Eight

1. National Center for Chronic Disease Prevention and Health Promotion (2005). *Youth online: Alcohol and other drug use,* From http://apps.nccd.cdc.gov. Retrieved October 4, 2007

Chapter Nine

1. J. Ortberg, *Everybody's Normal Till You Get to Know Them* (Grand Rapids, MI: Zondervan Publishing House, 2003).

2. Ibid., p. 163.

Chapter Ten

1. John Ortberg, *Love Beyond Reason: Moving God's Love from Your Head to Your Heart*, (Grand Rapids, MI: Zondervan Publishing House, 1998).

2. Ibid., p. 16.

Other Great Harvest House Books for Young Women

Set-Apart Femininity
Leslie Ludy

Author Leslie Ludy reveals how your pursuit of acceptance and sameness directly counters your true purpose—to be set apart by your love for God and God's love for you. This empowering message is filled with inspiring stories, personal illustrations, and a foundation of God's Word to awaken you to sacred femininity and a life infused with meaning. Each chapter encourages you to release worldly standards and set your sights on a more worthy pursuit. Surrender to God's love and wholeness, embrace the real blueprint for beauty, enjoy spectacular purpose, captivate the masculine heart, and cultivate spiritual strength. This journey will spark a desire in you to leave the fairy tale of the masses behind and walk toward the unique beauty, love, and dreams God has for you.

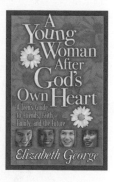

A Young Woman After God's Own Heart
Elizabeth George

Written by bestselling author and mentor Elizabeth George, this book will help you discover the intentions and blessings of God's heart. On this journey you'll learn about His priorities for your life—including prayer, submission, faithfulness, and joy—and how to embrace those priorities in daily life. Best of all, you'll discover that God is a faithful, caring, and loving presence during this exciting and sometimes difficult time of your life.

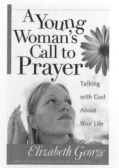

A Young Woman's Call to Prayer
Elizabeth George

From her own journey, the Bible, and the lives of others, author Elizabeth George reveals the explosive power and dynamic impact of prayer on everyday life. You will discover how to make prayer a reality, establish a regular time for talking with God, pray from your heart for daily needs, live God's will to the max, and worship God through prayer.